OFFICIAL PAST PAPERS WITH ANSWERS

INTERMEDIATE 1

CHEMISTRY
2008-2012

2008 EXAM — page 3
2009 EXAM — page 31
2010 EXAM — page 61
2011 EXAM — page 87
2012 EXAM — page 113
ANSWER SECTION — page 145

© Scottish Qualifications Authority
All rights reserved. Copying prohibited. No part of this publication may be reproduced, stored in a retrieval system, or transmitted in any form or by any means, electronic, mechanical, photocopying, recording or otherwise.

First exam published in 2008.
Published by Bright Red Publishing Ltd, 6 Stafford Street, Edinburgh EH3 7AU
tel: 0131 220 5804 fax: 0131 220 6710 info@brightredpublishing.co.uk www.brightredpublishing.co.uk

ISBN 978-1-84948-261-5

A CIP Catalogue record for this book is available from the British Library.

Bright Red Publishing is grateful to the copyright holders, as credited on the final page of the Question Section, for permission to use their material. Every effort has been made to trace the copyright holders and to obtain their permission for the use of copyright material. Bright Red Publishing will be happy to receive information allowing us to rectify any error or omission in future editions.

INTERMEDIATE 1
2008

OFFICIAL SQA PAST PAPERS | 5 | INTERMEDIATE 1 CHEMISTRY 2008

FOR OFFICIAL USE

Section B Total Marks

X012/101

NATIONAL QUALIFICATIONS 2008

FRIDAY, 30 MAY 9.00 AM – 10.30 AM

CHEMISTRY INTERMEDIATE 1

Fill in these boxes and read what is printed below.

Full name of centre

Town

Forename(s)

Surname

Date of birth
Day Month Year

Scottish candidate number

Number of seat

Necessary data will be found in the Chemistry Data Booklet for Intermediate 1 and Access 3 (2007 Edition).

Section A — Questions 1—20 (20 marks)

Instructions for completion of **Section A** are given on page two.

For this section of the examination you must use an **HB pencil**.

Section B (40 marks)

All questions should be attempted.

The questions may be answered in any order but all answers are to be written in this answer book, **and must be written clearly and legibly in ink**.

Rough work, if any should be necessary, should be written in this book, and then scored through when the fair copy has been written. If further space is required, a supplementary sheet for rough work may be obtained from the invigilator.

Additional space for answers will be found at the end of the book. If further space is required, supplementary sheets may be obtained from the invigilator and should be inserted inside the **front** cover of this booklet.

Before leaving the examination room you must give this book to the invigilator. If you do not, you may lose all the marks for this paper.

Read carefully

1. Check that the answer sheet provided is for **Chemistry Intermediate 1 (Section A)**.
2. For this section of the examination you must use an **HB pencil** and, where necessary, an eraser.
3. Check that the answer sheet you have been given has **your name**, **date of birth**, **SCN** (Scottish Candidate Number) and **Centre Name** printed on it.
   Do not change any of these details.
4. If any of this information is wrong, tell the Invigilator immediately.
5. If this information is correct, **print** your name and seat number in the boxes provided.
6. The answer to each question is **either** A, B, C or D. Decide what your answer is, then, using your pencil, put a horizontal line in the space provided (see sample question below).
7. There is **only one correct** answer to each question.
8. Any rough working should be done on the question paper or the rough working sheet, **not** on your answer sheet.
9. At the end of the exam, put the **answer sheet for Section A inside the front cover of this answer book**.

Sample Question

To show that the ink in a ball-pen consists of a mixture of dyes, the method of separation would be

A chromatography

B fractional distillation

C fractional crystallisation

D filtration.

The correct answer is **A**—chromatography. The answer **A** has been clearly marked in **pencil** with a horizontal line (see below).

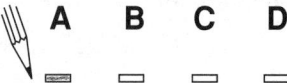

Changing an answer

If you decide to change your answer, carefully erase your first answer and using your pencil, fill in the answer you want. The answer below has been changed to **D**.

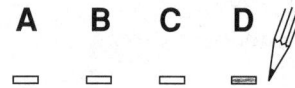

SECTION A

This section of the question paper consists of 20 multiple-choice questions.

1. Which hazard label would be used to show that an oven cleaner is **corrosive**?

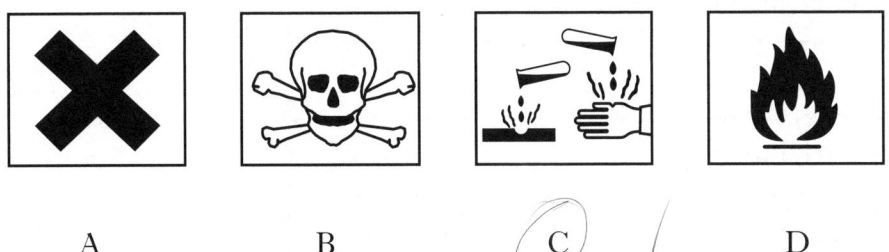

   A   B   C   D

2. Which of the following is an example of a chemical reaction?

   A   Petrol burning
   B   Nail varnish drying
   C   An ice cube melting
   D   Sugar dissolving in tea

3. Which of the following diagrams represents a mixture?

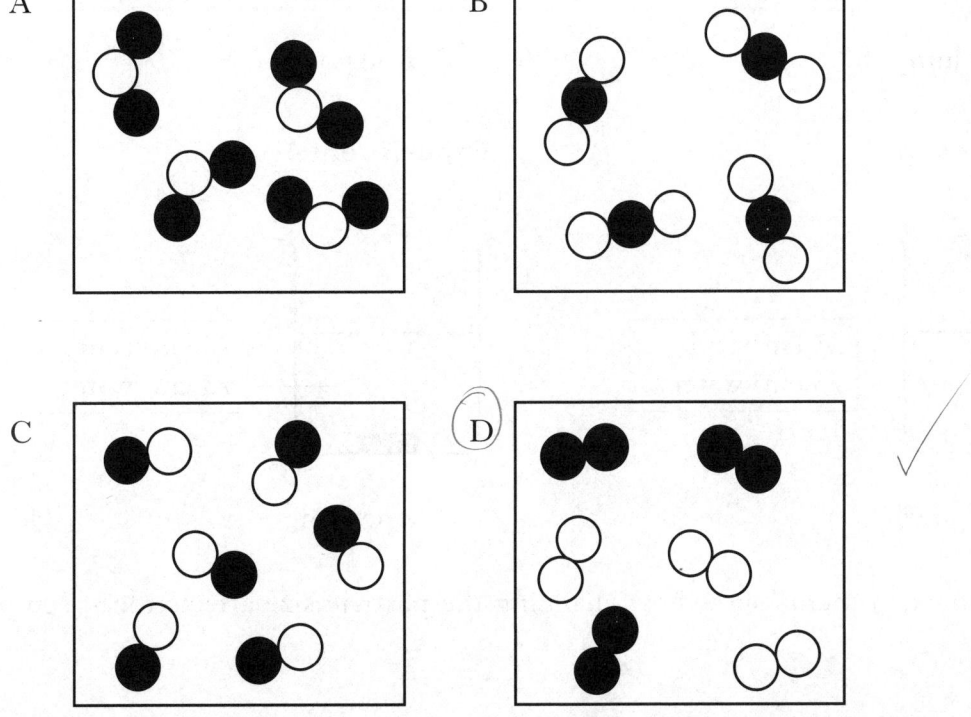

[Turn over

4. A student adds 1 gram of a catalyst to a reaction mixture.

Which line in the table shows what happens when the 1 gram of catalyst is added to the mixture?

	Speed of reaction	Mass of catalyst left at end in grams
A	unchanged	1
B	faster	1
C	unchanged	0
D	faster	0

5. A student set up four experiments to investigate the reaction between zinc and dilute hydrochloric acid.

Experiment 1

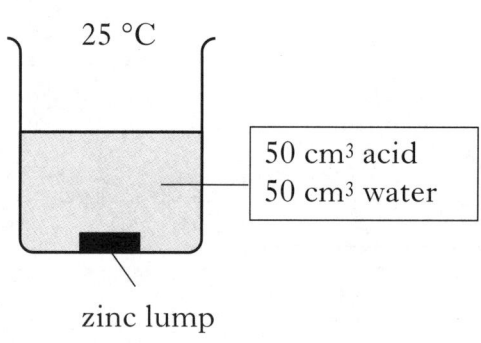

zinc lump

Experiment 2

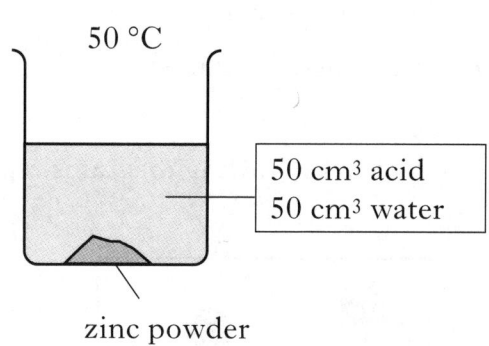

zinc powder

Experiment 3

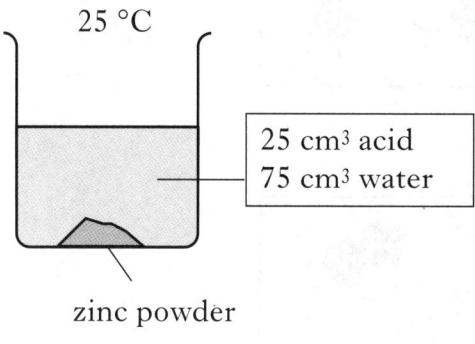

zinc powder

Experiment 4

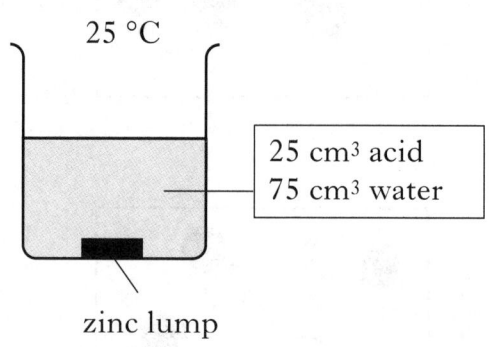

zinc lump

Which two experiments show how changing the particle size affects the speed of the reaction?

A 1 and 2

B 2 and 3

C 3 and 4

D 4 and 1

6. A nettle sting is acidic.

   Which of the following substances can neutralise a nettle sting?

   A Baking soda

   B Lemon juice

   C Soda water

   D Vinegar

7. Which of the following is formed when dilute nitric acid is added to potassium hydroxide solution?

   A Water

   B Oxygen

   C Hydrogen

   D Carbon dioxide

8. Which of the following metals is extracted from its ore using electricity?

   A Iron

   B Silver

   C Copper

   D Aluminium

9. Which gas burns with a "pop"?

   A Carbon dioxide

   B Hydrogen

   C Nitrogen

   D Oxygen

10. The corrosion of iron is also called

    A neutralisation

    B galvanising

    C combustion

    D rusting.

[Turn over

11. Which of the following would produce electricity?

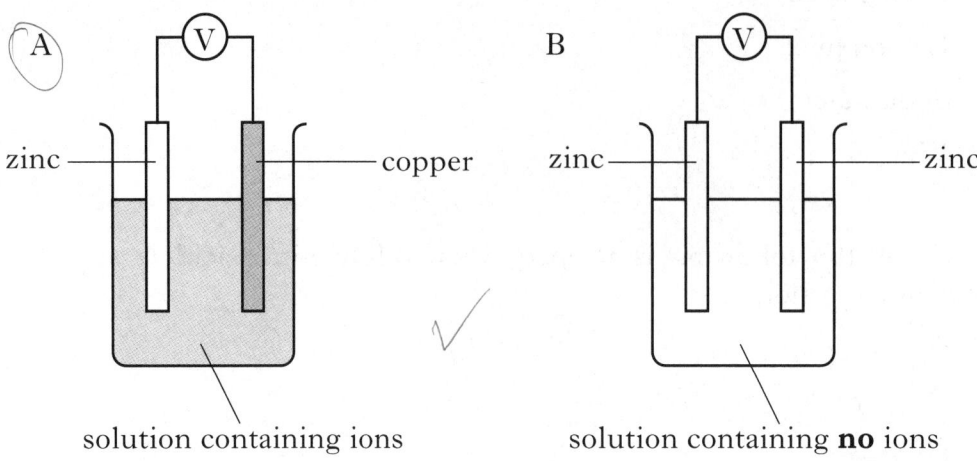

12. What substance is formed when soap is shaken with hard water?

  A Detergent
  B Grease
  C Scum
  D Shampoo

13. Which term describes the industrial method of producing shorter, more useful hydrocarbons from larger ones?

  A Cracking
  B Distillation
  C Evaporation
  D Filtration

14. Which property of PVC plastic makes it suitable for covering electrical wires?

- A   It is synthetic
- C   It is an electrical insulator
- B   It is washable
- D   It is thermoplastic

15. A herbicide is used to

- A   control plant pests
- B   kill weeds
- C   prevent plant disease
- D   replace essential elements in soil.

16. Which **three** elements are essential for healthy plant growth?

- A   Calcium, nitrogen and potassium
- B   Calcium, phosphorus and potassium
- C   Nitrogen, phosphorus and calcium
- D   Nitrogen, phosphorus and potassium

17. Animals obtain energy by respiration.

During respiration

- A   carbon dioxide is used up
- B   glucose is used up
- C   oxygen is produced
- D   starch is produced.

[Turn over

18. Which of the following should be used to show that carbon dioxide is produced during fermentation?

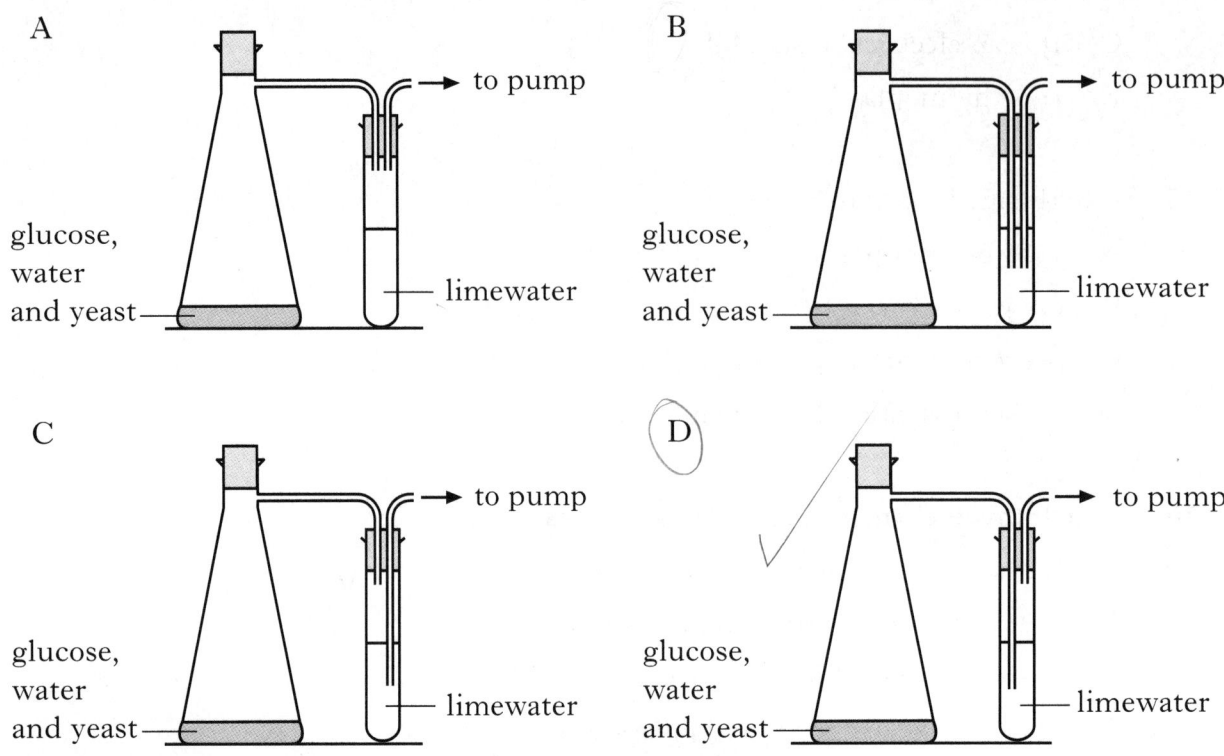

19. The graph shows how the alcohol level in a man's body changes with time.

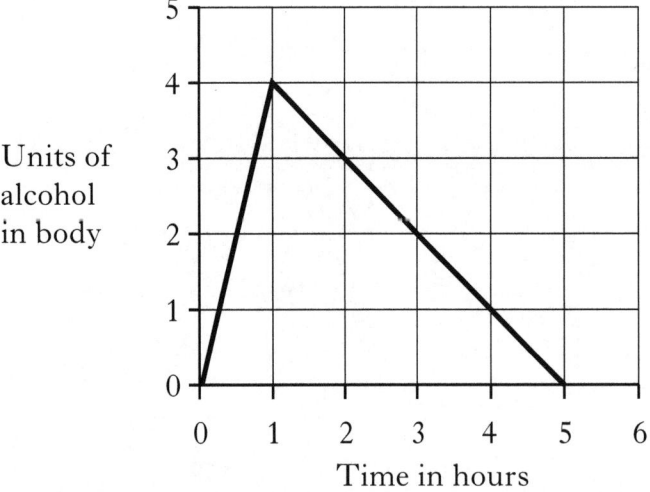

During the first hour, the man drank

A 1 pint of beer

B 2 glasses of wine

C 2 bottles of alcopop

D 3 measures of spirit.

20. The table shows the number of drug-related deaths in Scotland over a five-year period.

Year	Number of drug-related deaths
1	153
2	209
3	247
4	251
5	267

Over the five-year period, the table shows that

A the number of drug-related deaths increases

B the number of drug-related deaths decreases

C the number of drug-related deaths stays constant

D there is no general trend in the number of drug-related deaths.

Candidates are reminded that the answer sheet MUST be returned INSIDE this answer book.

[Turn over for Section B on *Page ten*

SECTION B

40 marks are available in this section of the paper.

All answers must be written clearly and legibly in ink.

1. Elements are listed in the Periodic Table.

   (a) Each element has a name and a chemical symbol.

   Write the chemical symbol for the element magnesium.

   (You may wish to use page 1 of the data booklet to help you.)

   Mg

   (b) Each element has an atomic number.

   Name the element which has an atomic number of **6**.

   (You may wish to use page 1 of the data booklet to help you.)

   Carbon

   (c) Each element is made up of atoms.

   Atoms contain particles called protons and neutrons.

   Use the following information to complete the table for the element sodium.

Number of protons = atomic number
Number of protons + neutrons = mass number

Atomic number	11
Number of protons	11
Number of neutrons	12
Mass number	23

2. Water from reservoirs needs to be treated before it can be used in the home. The table shows the reason for each treatment.

Treatment	Reason
clarification	to remove suspended solids
filtration	to remove undissolved solids
disinfection	to kill bacteria

(a) During clarification, sodium aluminate is added to the water.

Sodium aluminate contains aluminium and **two** other elements.

Name the two other elements.

Sodium and oxygen

(b) Filtration is used by water companies to remove solids.

The filters used can be made from poly(propene).

Name the monomer used to make poly(propene).

propene

(c) Name the element which can be used as a disinfectant to kill bacteria.

chlorine

[Turn over

3. Milk is made up of mainly protein, fat, sugar and water.

A method which is used to find the mass of solids present in milk is shown.

50 grams of milk is weighed out. The milk is heated to dryness and then left to cool. The mass of solid remaining can then be measured.

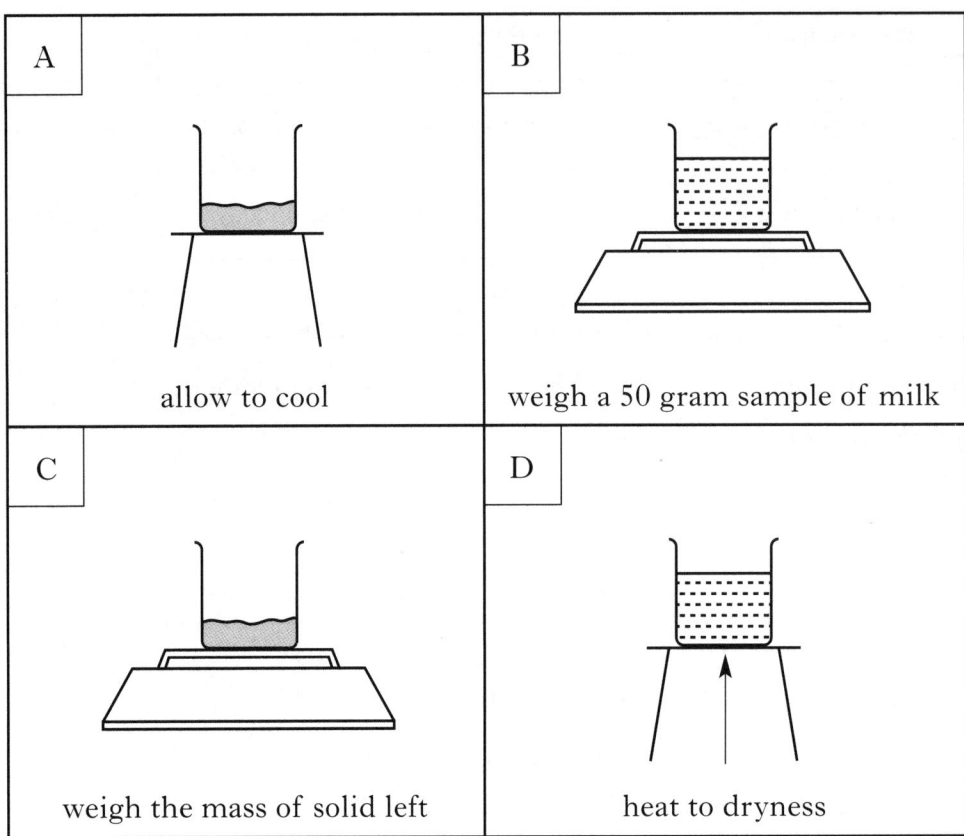

(a) Place a letter in each box to show the order in which the experiment is carried out.

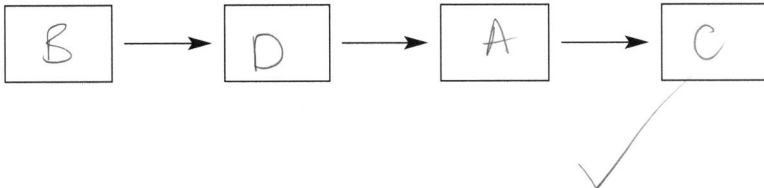

3. **(continued)**

(b) Benedict's solution can be used to test for sugars in milk.

The **PPA "Testing for Starch and Sugars in Food"** gives a method for this test.

	Method
Step 1	Pour some milk into a test tube.
Step 2	Add Benedict's solution to the test tube containing the milk.
Step 3	_See a colour change if sugar is present._ ✗

(i) Complete step 3. **1**

(ii) When Benedict's solution is added to milk a colour change takes place. What colour change would be seen?

Blue ⟶ _red_ ✓ **1**

(3)

[Turn over

4. An alloy of aluminium is used in the manufacture of the European Airbus.

The table shows the elements present in the alloy.

Elements present in the alloy				
aluminium	copper	magnesium	silicon	iron

(a) Name the element present in the alloy which is **not** a metal.

(You may wish to use page 1 of the data booklet to help you.)

silicon

(b) What property of aluminium makes it suitable to be used in the manufacture of aircraft bodies?

(You may wish to use page 5 of the data booklet to help you.)

low density

4. (continued)

(c) A student sets up the circuit below to test the electrical conductivity of aluminium and other elements.

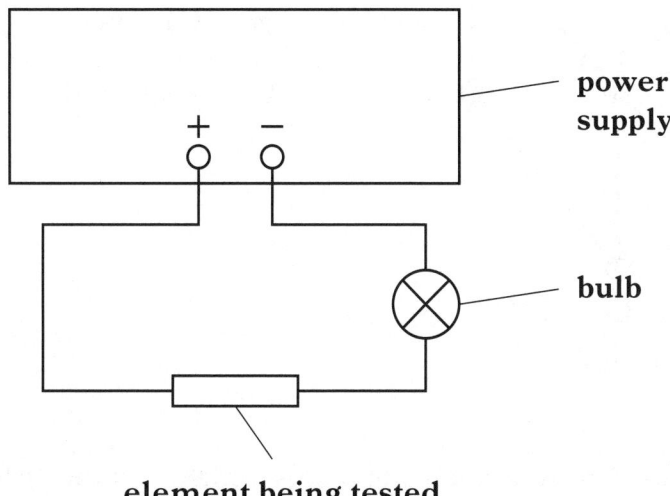

(i) What would be **seen** if the element conducts electricity?

The bulb would light up.

(ii) Complete the table for the other elements.

Element	Conductor/Non-conductor
aluminium	conductor
sulphur	non conductor
tin	conductor

(You may wish to use page 1 of the data booklet to help you.)

5. Cubane is a compound of carbon and hydrogen that can be used as an explosive.

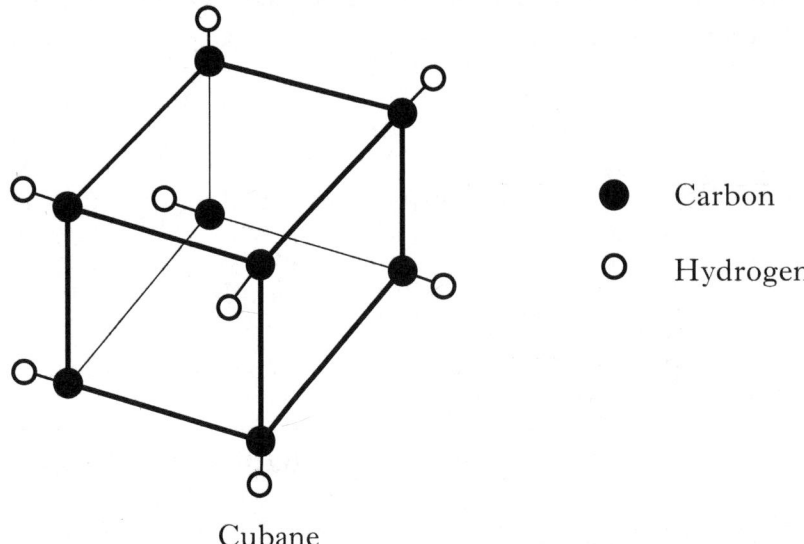

Cubane

(a) What term is used to describe compounds which contain carbon and hydrogen only?

hydrocarbon

(b) The table shows the melting point of cubane and other carbon compounds.

Name of Compound	Molecular Formula	Melting point (°C)
Cubane	C_8H_8	130
Octane	C_8H_{18}	-57
Cycloctane	C_8H_{16}	14
Octene	C_8H_{16}	-102

(i) Complete the table by adding the molecular formula of cubane.

(ii) What is unusual about the melting point of cubane, when it is compared to the other melting points in the table?

It has the highest melting point despite having the same amount of carbons and least amount of hydrogens.

6. Shampoos contain different types of chemicals.

The three main types of chemicals, and their uses, are shown in the chart.

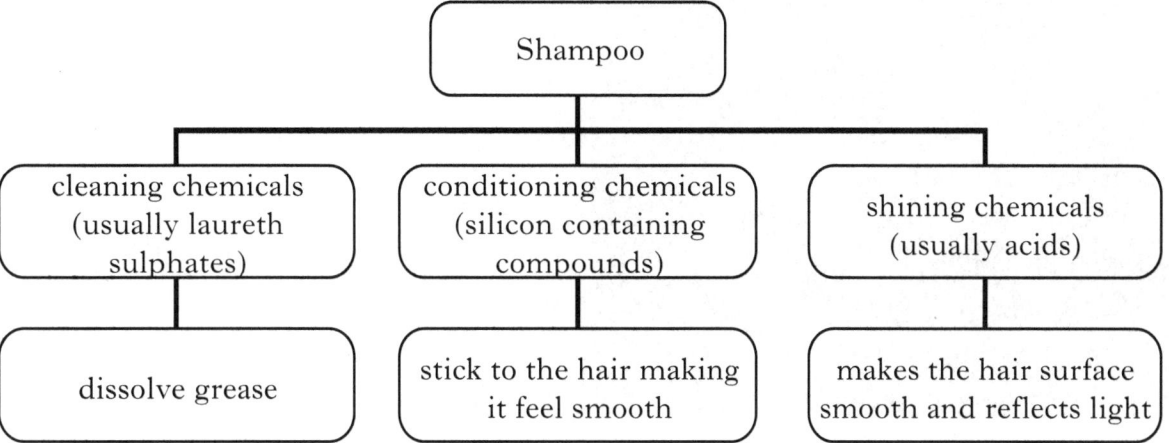

Use the information in the chart to answer the following questions.

(a) Why do **cleaning** chemicals in shampoo remove grease from hair?

They dissolve grease. ✓   1

(b) Shampoos contain chemicals to make the hair shine.

Suggest a pH value for these chemicals.

1–6. ✓   1

(c) The label shows the ingredients in a shampoo.

Identify an ingredient which could be a **cleaning** chemical.

sodium laureth sulphate ✓   1

(3)

7. Coal is used as a fuel.

(a) When coal burns energy is released.

Name the gas needed for coal to burn.

oxygen

(b) Coal contains mainly carbon.

The table shows the percentage of carbon in different types of coal.

Type of coal	Percentage of carbon
lignite	50
bituminous	65
anthracite	90

(i) When it is burned, anthracite produces more energy than the other two types of coal.

Suggest a reason for this.

It has a higher percentage of carbon

DO NOT WRITE IN THIS MARGIN

Marks

7. (*b*) (continued)

(ii) Calculate the mass of carbon present in 200 kilograms of anthracite.

Show your working clearly.

anthracite 90% carbon

200kg of anthracite

10% of 200 = 2

2 × 9 = 18

18 × 10 = 180

180 kilograms. **1**

(*c*) Coal is a finite resource.

What is meant by a finite resource?

It will run out

1

(4)

[Turn over

8. The table shows the percentage of each type of waste in an average household.

Type of waste	Percentage of household waste
paper and card	25
waste plant material	15
plastic	10
glass	10 ✓
other	40

(a) Complete the table to show the percentage of waste from glass.

(b) The pie chart shows the information from the table.

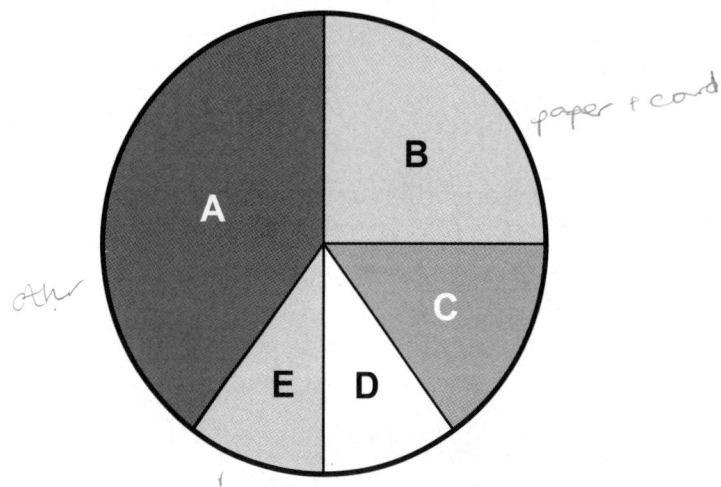

(i) Which letter shows waste due to paper and card?

Letter ___B___ ✓

(ii) Identify the type of waste shown as C in the pie chart.

___waste plant material___ ✓

DO NOT WRITE IN THIS MARGIN

Marks

8. (continued)

(*c*) Household waste can be disposed of in a variety of ways.

(i) Name one type of waste which can be recycled.

plastic ✓ **1**

(ii) Waste plant material can decompose to produce a gas. This gas is used as a renewable energy source.

Name this gas.

methane ✓ **1**

(5)

[Turn over

9. Read the following passage and answer the questions.

> All additives used in foodstuffs must be safe. Many foods go off quickly without the use of preservatives. It is now known that preservatives prevent the growth of micro-organisms, some of which are extremely dangerous.
>
> Most preservatives are simple chemicals and are closely related to natural substances. For example, benzoic acid occurs in several fruits and is widely used in fruit preservation. Sorbic acid, another preservative, is an unsaturated acid found in some plants.
>
> Some preservatives have been used for hundreds of years. For example wood smoke is used to preserve fish. However, wood smoke contains a large number of hydrocarbons, some of which cause cancer.

Adapted from *In the Mix* by Food Additives and Ingredients Association.

(a) Why are preservatives added to food?

To prevent the growth of micro-organisms

(b) Name the unsaturated acid found in some plants.

Sorbic acid

(c) Which compounds present in wood smoke may cause cancer?

hydrocarbons

(d) Sulphur dioxide is another widely used preservative.

Write the formula for sulphur dioxide.

Sulpher + Oxygen → sulpher dioxide

10. The table shows the nutritional information of a burger.

Class of food	Protein	Carbohydrate	Fat	Fibre
Mass in grams per 100 grams	15·0	18·2	13·0	1·8

(a) (i) Why are carbohydrate and fat needed by the body?

produce energy ✓

(ii) In 100 grams of a burger there are 13 grams of fat.

Why are people encouraged to eat less fat?

It can be bad for your health. Can damage your heart. ✓

(b) (i) Why must fibre be included in the diet?

to keep the gut working ✓

(ii) A burger was found to contain 30 grams of protein.

What is the mass of fibre in a 200 gram burger?

1·8 + 1·8 = 3·6

3·6 grams

(4)

[Turn over

11. Plants such as elodea are placed in fish tanks to supply oxygen.

They produce oxygen by photosynthesis.

(a) What type of energy is needed for photosynthesis to take place?

light

(b) Complete the word equation for photosynthesis.

Carbon dioxide + water ⟶ glucose + oxygen

(c) The graph shows how the solubility of oxygen in water changes with temperature.

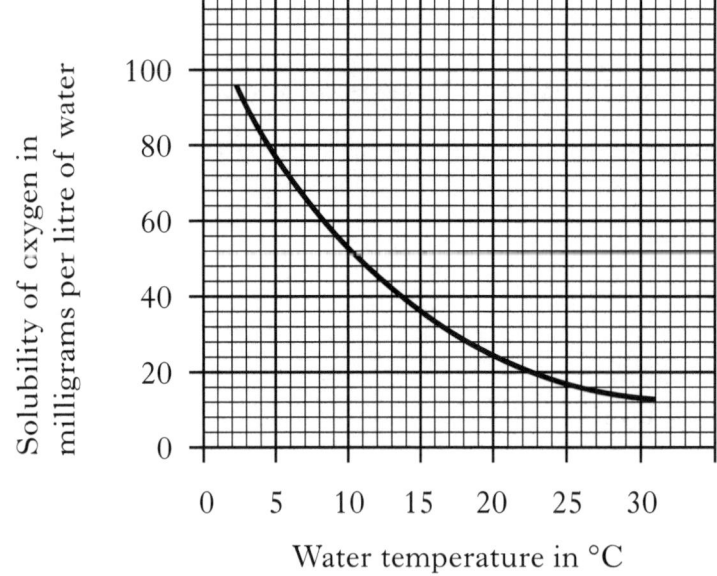

Use the graph to complete the following sentence.

As the temperature of the water increases, the solubility of oxygen

decreases.

[END OF QUESTION PAPER]

ADDITIONAL SPACE FOR ANSWERS

ADDITIONAL SPACE FOR ANSWERS

INTERMEDIATE 1
2009

[BLANK PAGE]

OFFICIAL SQA PAST PAPERS 33 INTERMEDIATE 1 CHEMISTRY 2009

FOR OFFICIAL USE

Section B Total Marks

X012/101

NATIONAL QUALIFICATIONS 2009

WEDNESDAY, 3 JUNE 9.00 AM – 10.30 AM

CHEMISTRY INTERMEDIATE 1

Fill in these boxes and read what is printed below.

Full name of centre

Town

Forename(s)

Surname

Date of birth
Day Month Year

Scottish candidate number

Number of seat

Necessary data will be found in the Chemistry Data Booklet for Intermediate 1 and Access 3.

Section A — Questions 1—20 (20 marks)

Instructions for completion of **Section A** are given on page two.

For this section of the examination you must use an **HB pencil**.

Section B (40 marks)

All questions should be attempted.

The questions may be answered in any order but all answers are to be written in this answer book, **and must be written clearly and legibly in ink**.

Rough work, if any should be necessary, should be written in this book, and then scored through when the fair copy has been written. If further space is required, a supplementary sheet for rough work may be obtained from the invigilator.

Additional space for answers will be found at the end of the book. If further space is required, supplementary sheets may be obtained from the invigilator and should be inserted inside the **front** cover of this booklet.

Before leaving the examination room you must give this book to the invigilator. If you do not, you may lose all the marks for this paper.

Read carefully

1. Check that the answer sheet provided is for **Chemistry Intermediate 1 (Section A)**.
2. For this section of the examination you must use an **HB pencil** and, where necessary, an eraser.
3. Check that the answer sheet you have been given has **your name**, **date of birth**, **SCN** (Scottish Candidate Number) and **Centre Name** printed on it.
   Do not change any of these details.
4. If any of this information is wrong, tell the Invigilator immediately.
5. If this information is correct, **print** your name and seat number in the boxes provided.
6. The answer to each question is **either** A, B, C or D. Decide what your answer is, then, using your pencil, put a horizontal line in the space provided (see sample question below).
7. There is **only one correct** answer to each question.
8. Any rough working should be done on the question paper or the rough working sheet, **not** on your answer sheet.
9. At the end of the exam, put the **answer sheet for Section A inside the front cover of this answer book**.

Sample Question

To show that the ink in a ball-pen consists of a mixture of dyes, the method of separation would be

A chromatography

B fractional distillation

C fractional crystallisation

D filtration.

The correct answer is **A**—chromatography. The answer **A** has been clearly marked in **pencil** with a horizontal line (see below).

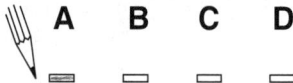

Changing an answer

If you decide to change your answer, carefully erase your first answer and using your pencil, fill in the answer you want. The answer below has been changed to **D**.

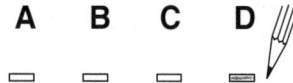

SECTION A

This section of the question paper consists of 20 multiple-choice questions.

1. The diagram shows part of the Periodic Table.

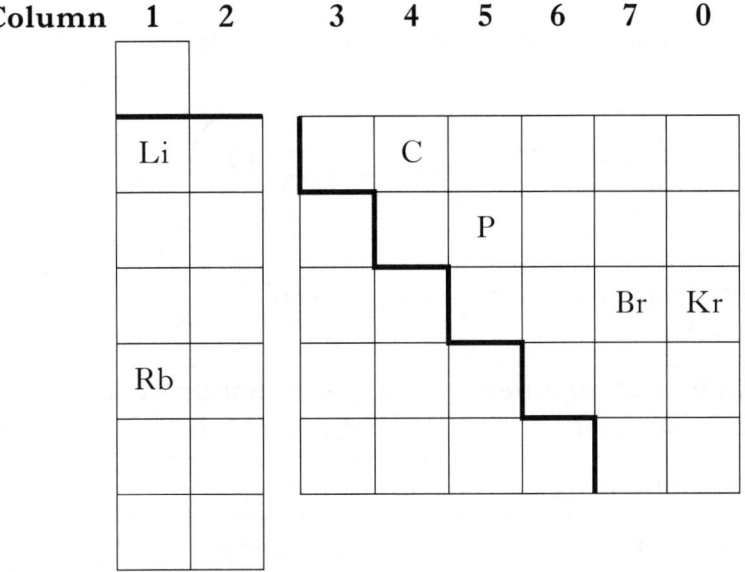

Which **two** elements show similar chemical properties?

A Li and C

B C and P

C Br and Kr

D Li and Rb

2. Which of the following cylinders contains a mixture of gases?

A 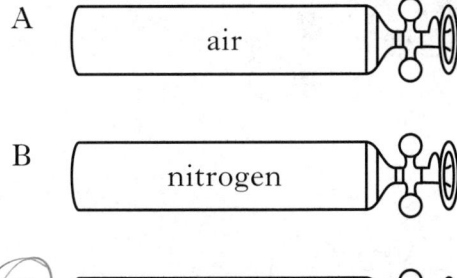 air

B nitrogen

C 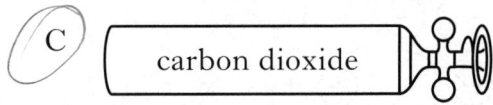 carbon dioxide

D 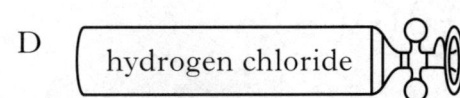 hydrogen chloride

[Turn over

3. Which of the following compounds contains oxygen?

   A Calcium chloride

   B Lithium sulphide

   C Potassium nitrate

   D Sodium chloride

4. The diagram below shows a molecule of carbon dioxide.

   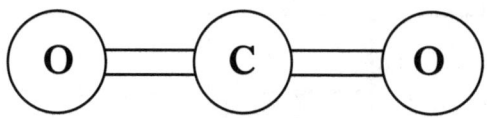

   Which line in the table is correct for this molecule?

	Particles joined together in the molecule	Strength of bonds inside the molecule
A	atoms	weak
B	atoms	strong
C	ions	weak
D	ions	strong

5. The structures of substances can be represented by models.

   Which of the following models shows an element?

   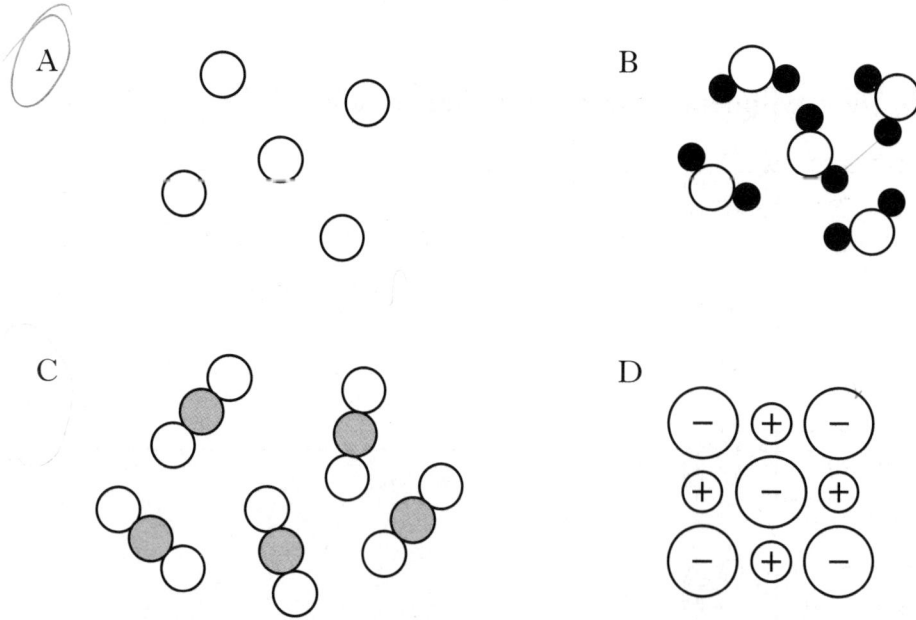

6. The formula for dinitrogen monoxide is

   A NO

   B NO_2

   C N_2O

   D N_2O_4.

7. The rusting of iron is also called

   A corrosion

   B combustion

   C fermentation

   D neutralisation.

8. Detergents are able to break up grease and oil into tiny droplets which can then mix with water.

   This happens because

   A detergents are soluble in oil only

   B detergents are soluble in water only

   C detergents are soluble in oil and water

   D detergents are insoluble in oil and water.

9. Which of the following is a synthetic fibre?

   A Cotton

   B Nylon

   C Silk

   D Wool

10. Which of the following is a renewable fuel?

    A Coal

    B Petrol

    C Diesel

    D Ethanol

[Turn over

11. Which line in the table shows the plastic that is best suited for use in bullet-proof vests?

	Plastic	Property
A	Kevlar	very strong
B	PVC	flexible
C	Formica	high melting point
D	Perspex	lets light through

12. Polythene is a plastic which can be heated and re-shaped. Bacteria can **not** break it down.

Polythene can be described as

A thermosetting and biodegradable

B thermosetting and non-biodegradable

C thermoplastic and biodegradable

D thermoplastic and non-biodegradable.

13. Polymers can be made by joining together small molecules called monomers.

Which of the following is a monomer?

A Bakelite

B Ethene

C Nylon

D Perspex

14. In sunlight, a reaction takes place in green plants.

In this reaction, carbon dioxide and water change into glucose and a gas.

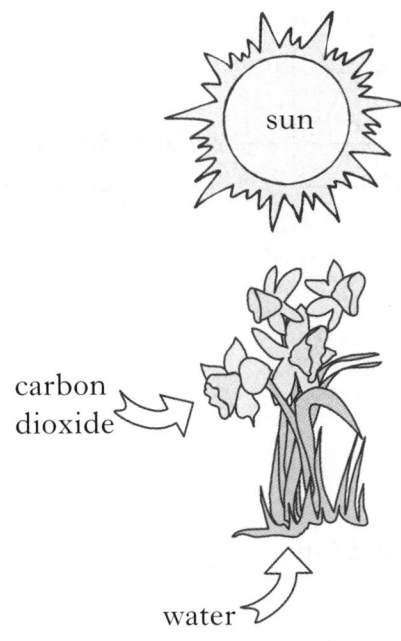

What is the name for this reaction?

A Combustion

B Respiration

C Fermentation

D Photosynthesis

15. Which gas in the atmosphere is responsible for the greenhouse effect?

A Carbon dioxide

B Nitrogen

C Oxygen

D Argon

16. Which line in the table shows a compound which could be used as a fertiliser?

Compound	Elements present	Solubility in water
A	sodium, chlorine, oxygen	soluble
B	calcium, sulphur, oxygen	soluble
C	sodium, nitrogen, oxygen	soluble
D	calcium, phosphorus, oxygen	insoluble

17. Which sugar does **not** give a brick-red colour when tested with Benedict's solution?

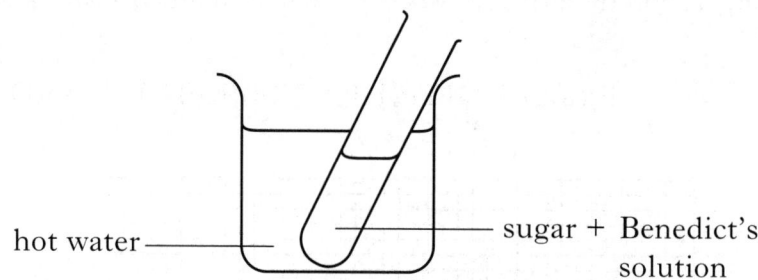

- A Maltose
- B Sucrose
- C Glucose
- D Fructose

18. Which of the following classes of food keeps the gut working well?
    - A Carbohydrate
    - B Fat
    - C Fibre
    - D Protein

19. Which of the following drinks contains the most units of alcohol?

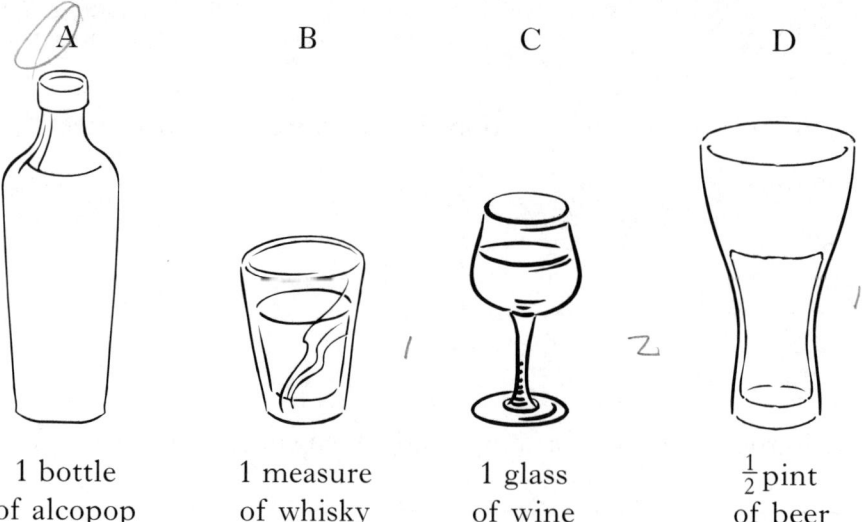

20. The most accurate term used to describe a chemical which fights micro-organisms is

A alcohol

B a drug

C a medicine

D an antibiotic.

Candidates are reminded that the answer sheet MUST be returned INSIDE this answer book.

[Turn over for Section B on *Page ten*

SECTION B

40 marks are available in this section of the paper.

All answers must be written clearly and legibly in ink.

1. Ozone forms naturally in the upper atmosphere from oxygen molecules. It protects the Earth from harmful UV radiation and is known as the ozone layer.

   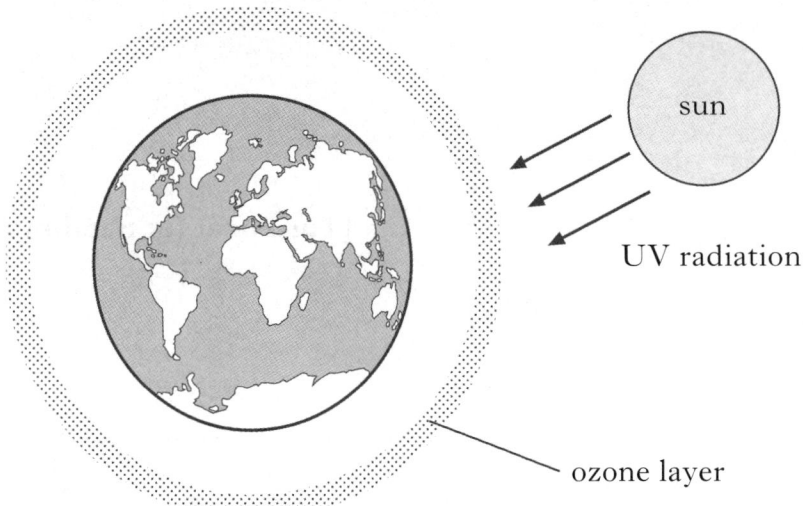

   (a) The diagram shows a molecule of ozone.

   Ozone

   Write the molecular formula for ozone.

   <u> O_3 </u>

   (b) The following hazard symbols would be found on a container of ozone. Name each hazard.

   <u> toxic </u>   <u> harmful </u>

1. **(continued)**

   (c) Sunscreens protect skin by absorbing UV radiation.

   There are three types of UV radiation: UVA, UVB and UVC.

   The graphs show how three sunscreens absorb UV radiation.

   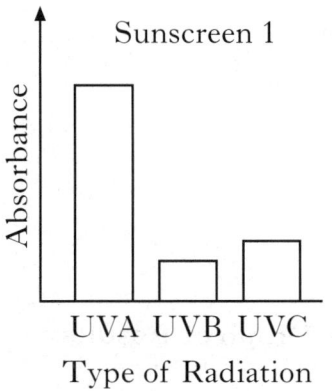
   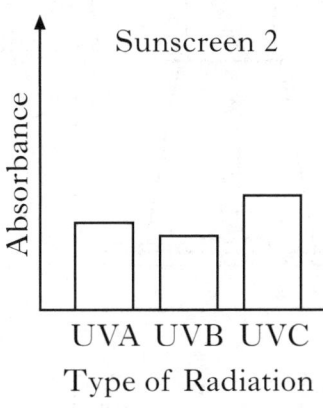
   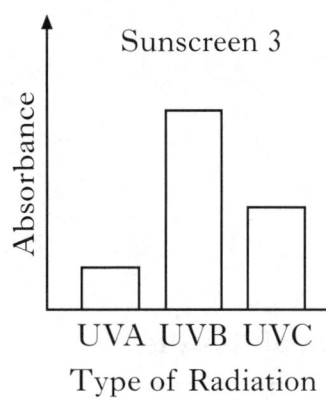

   UVB radiation causes the skin to go red.

   Which of these sunscreens would be best at stopping the skin from going red?

   Sunscreen 1

   1
   (3)

   [Turn over

2. Pure water boils at 100 °C.

The following equipment was used to investigate the effect that adding salt has on the boiling point of water.

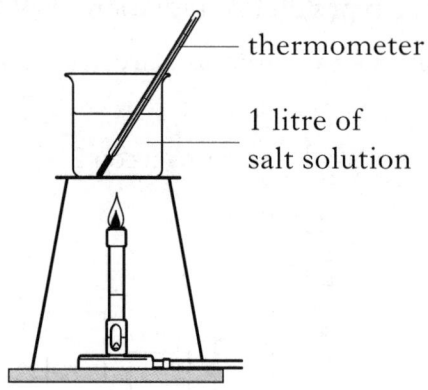

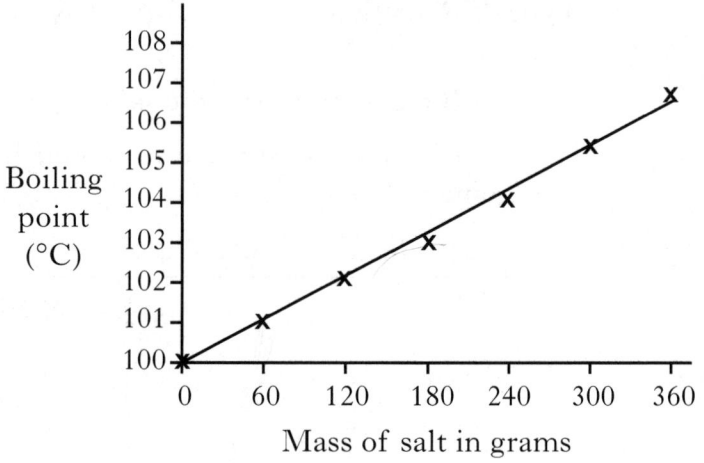

Table of Results

	Boiling point (°C)
0	100
60	101
120	102
180	103
240	104
300	105
360	106

Graph of Results

(a) Use the graph to complete the table of results by adding the missing heading.

(b) By how much is the boiling point of water **raised** when 60 g of salt is added?

_____1_____ °C

(c) When 420 g of salt is added not all of the salt dissolves.

Complete the sentence.

When no more salt will dissolve, a __Saturated__ solution has been formed.

3. The table shows the pH values of some common solutions.

Solutions	pH
wine	3
lemonade	4
black coffee	7
baking soda	9
bleach	12

(a) Name the **two** acids.

lemonade and *wine* 1

(b) Name the solution which is neutral.

black coffee 1

(c) When acids react with alkalis, salts are formed.

A student carried out a **PPA** to investigate the solubility of some salts.

The results are shown.

Name of salt	Soluble/Insoluble
ammonium sulphate	soluble
ammonium phosphate	soluble
calcium phosphate	insoluble
potassium nitrate	soluble
sodium nitrate	soluble

(i) What did the student **see** at the end of the experiment that showed calcium phosphate is insoluble?

It did not dissolve. 1

(ii) Name the acid that could be used to make the salt potassium nitrate.

_____ 1

(4)

4. Carbon dioxide gas can be used in fire extinguishers.

A student set up the following experiment to show that carbon dioxide gas can put out a flame.

(a) Complete the word equation to show the reactants and the third product.

| sodium carbonate lumps | + | dilute hydrochloric acid | → | sodium chloride | + | water | + | oxygen |

(b) A fire triangle shows what is needed for burning.

(i) Which part of the fire triangle is removed by carbon dioxide gas?

oxygen

(ii) State another name for burning.

Combustion

5. Crude oil is a mixture of hydrocarbons which can be separated into different fractions.

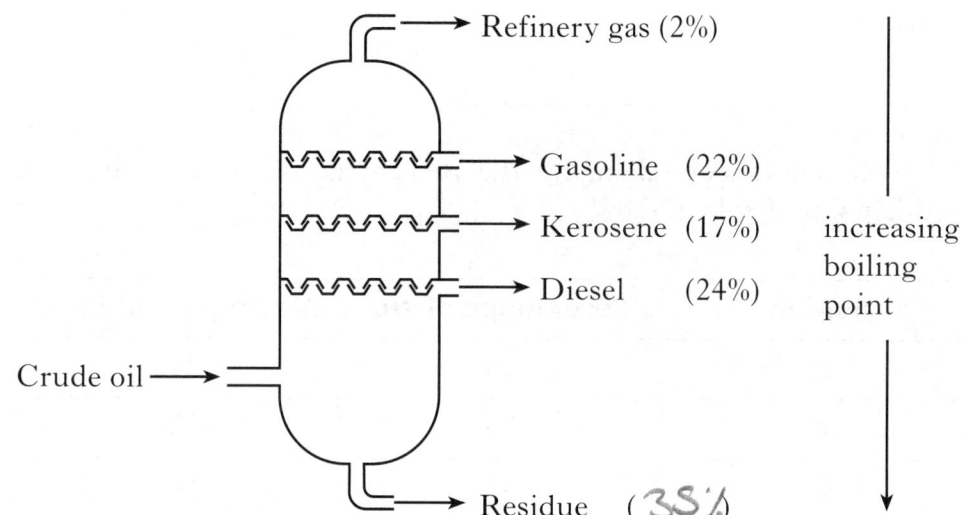

(a) Name the process used to separate crude oil into fractions.

   cracking

(b) The fractions contain hydrocarbons.

   Name the elements present in hydrocarbons.

   hydrogen carbon

(c) Complete the sentence by circling the correct word.

   The gasoline fraction boils at a [higher ~~lower~~] temperature than those in the kerosene fraction. The molecules in the gasoline fraction are [~~smaller~~ larger] than those in the kerosene fraction.

(d) Calculate the percentage of crude oil that remains as residue.

   _35_ %

```
  24
  22
+ 17
  02
  ──
  65
```

100 − 65 = 35

6. Solder is a mixture of tin and lead.

(a) What name is given to materials, such as solder, which are a mixture of metals?

Alloy

(b) The table shows how changing the percentage of tin can alter the melting point of solder.

Solder	Percentage of tin	Melting point in °C
A	40	260
B	50	227
C	67	190

(i) What effect does increasing the percentage of tin have on the melting point of solder?

It decreases

(ii) Another type of solder contains 55% tin.

Predict the temperature at which this solder will melt.

_240_ °C

(c) 'Tin-lead' solder is now being replaced by solder that does not contain lead.

Suggest a reason for replacing the lead used in solder.

It is toxic

7. A student investigated how well metals can react with oxygen.

The apparatus used is shown.

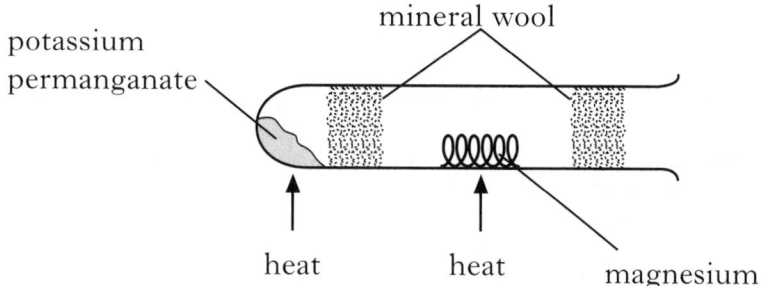

(a) Potassium permanganate releases oxygen when heated.

State the chemical test for oxygen.

Relights a glowing splint. **1**

(b) Three metals were tested.

(i) Complete the table to show the results for magnesium.

(You may wish to use page 6 of the data booklet to help you.)

Metal	Observation
copper	Dull red glow
magnesium	*bright white glow*
zinc	Bright red glow

1

(ii) Name a metal which would **not** react with oxygen.

(You may wish to use page 6 of the data booklet to help you.)

1

(3)

no bode

[Turn over

8. In the **PPA "Factors which affect Lathering"**, one factor which is investigated is the volume of detergent used.

The table shows the height of the lather obtained when different volumes of detergent were used.

Experiment	Height of lather in centimetres	
	First attempt	Second attempt
1	0·3	0·2
2	0·4	0·4
3	0·8	1·0

(a) During the investigation the volume of detergent was changed.

Describe how this was done.

By increasing the amount of detergant and keeping the volume the same 1

(b) Why was each experiment repeated?

to check it was correct 1

(c) In hard water areas, detergents are used because soap does not form a lather.

What forms when soap is used with hard water?

A scum. 1

(3)

9. Vitamins and minerals are substances which are required to keep the body healthy.

(a) Name an element found in milk and dairy products required by the body to keep bones strong.

Calcium

(b) **Vitamin D** is needed by people to strengthen their bones. Sunlight is needed for the body to make **vitamin D**. **Vitamin D** is also found in dairy products.

Vitamin A is important for our eyes. It protects their surface and helps us see in dim light. The best source of **vitamin A** is fish liver oil. The body can also get **vitamin A** by eating carrots – the orange substance in carrots (called carotene) is turned into **vitamin A** by the body.

Scurvy, a skin disease, is caused by a lack of **vitamin C**. **Vitamin C** is found in green vegetables and citrus fruits such as lemons and limes.

Vitamin B2, which is found in dairy products, is also needed for healthy skin.

(i) Use the information above to complete the following key by entering the names of the vitamins in the correct boxes.

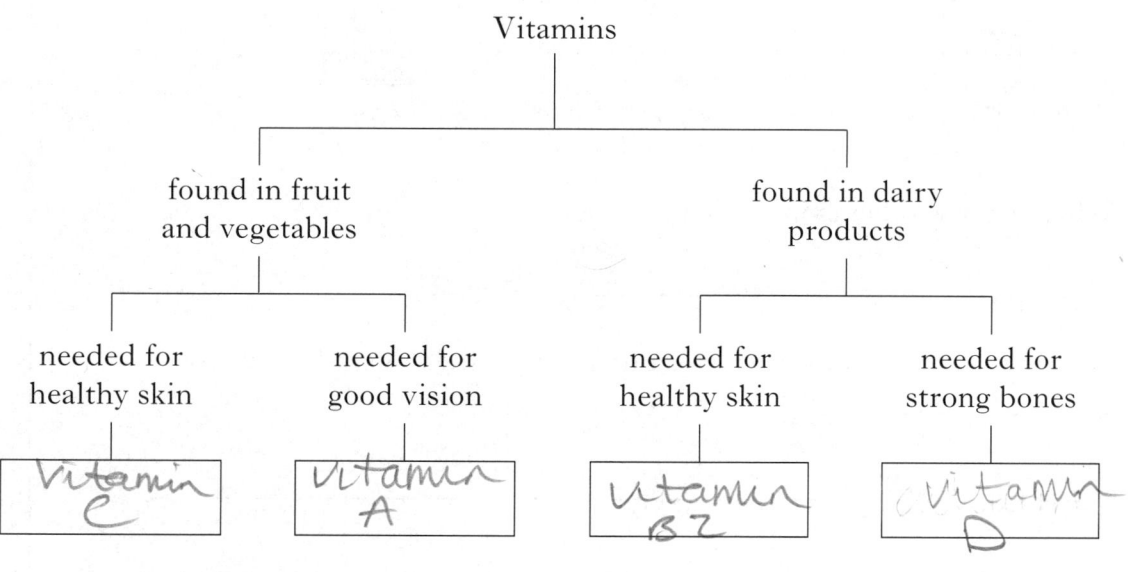

(ii) Name **two** vitamins which the body can make itself.

vitamin _D_   vitamin _A_

10. Sugar, flour, water and yeast are used to make dough for bread. Carbon dioxide is produced in the reaction which is catalysed by enzymes in yeast. The carbon dioxide causes the dough to rise.

The following experiment was used to investigate this.

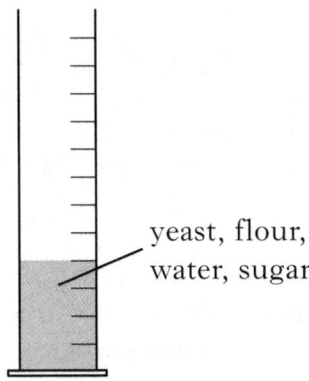

(a) The experiment was carried out under different conditions.

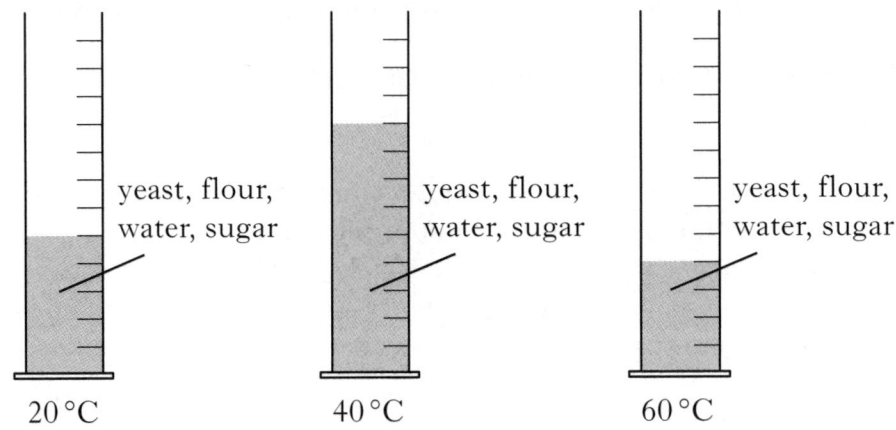

What factor was being investigated?

To see how the temperature effects the change

(b) When the experiment was carried out at 60 °C, the dough did not rise.

Suggest a reason for this.

It was too hot.

(2)

11. In the **PPA**, **"Burning Carbohydrates"**, the heat energy given out by burning different carbohydrates is compared.

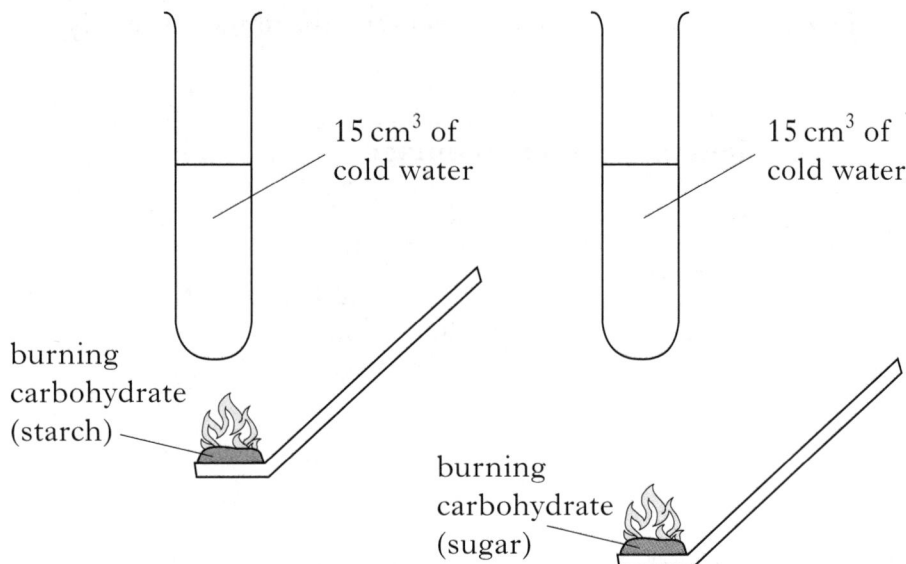

(a) Name the piece of equipment which is needed to allow the student to compare the heat energy released.

A thermometer.

(b) Why can this experiment **not** be described as a fair test?

They use a different substance.

12. As well as carbohydrates, a bar of chocolate contains minerals, protein and fat.

(a) The table shows the elements present in the minerals in a bar of chocolate. The percentages of each element in the minerals is also shown.

Element	Percentage
magnesium	25
phosphorus	10
iron	20
zinc	8
calcium	2

(i) Name the non-metal found in the minerals in the bar of chocolate.

calcium

(ii) Use the information in the table to:
- label and complete the scale on the vertical axis;
- draw a bar graph of the results.

(Additional graph paper, if required, can be found on page 24.)

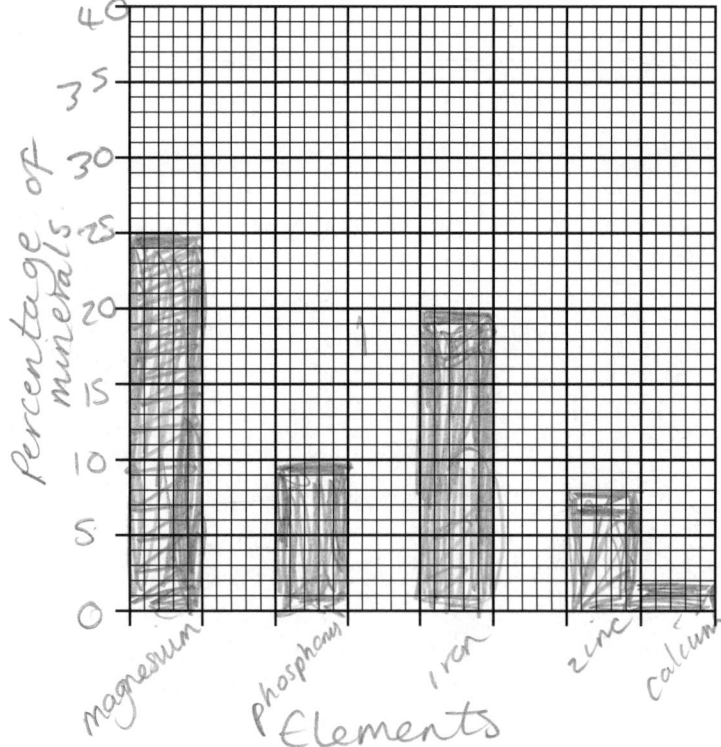

12. (continued)

(b) The protein present in the bar of chocolate reacts with soda lime and a gas is given off.

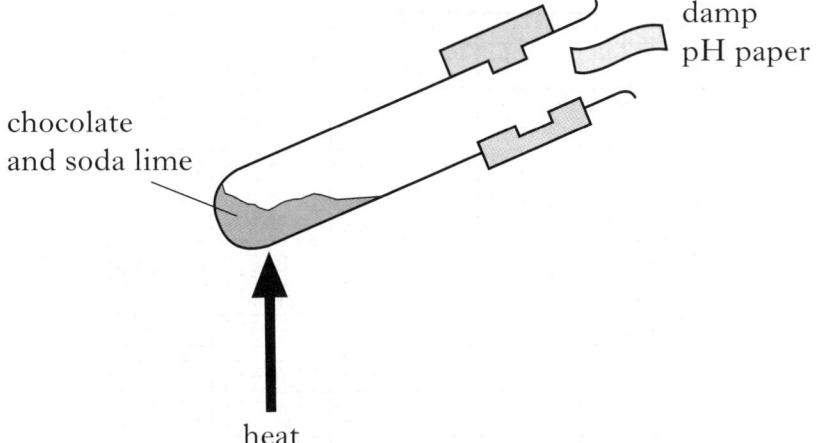

What colour would the damp pH paper turn?

Yellow   1

(c) How would you show that chocolate also contains fat?

It would leave grease   1

(5)

[END OF QUESTION PAPER]

ADDITIONAL SPACE FOR ANSWERS

ADDITIONAL GRAPH PAPER FOR QUESTION 12(*a*)(ii).

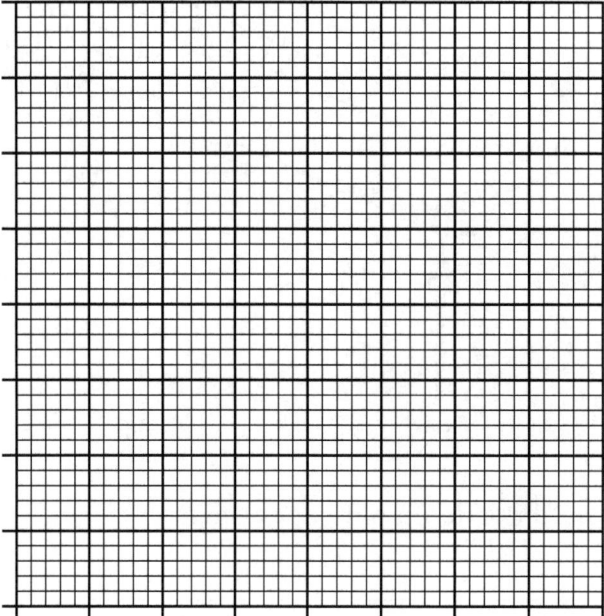

ADDITIONAL SPACE FOR ANSWERS

ADDITIONAL SPACE FOR ANSWERS

ADDITIONAL SPACE FOR ANSWERS

INTERMEDIATE 1

2010

[BLANK PAGE]

OFFICIAL SQA PAST PAPERS 63 INTERMEDIATE 1 CHEMISTRY 2010

FOR OFFICIAL USE

Section B Total Marks

X012/101

NATIONAL QUALIFICATIONS 2010

WEDNESDAY, 2 JUNE 9.00 AM – 10.30 AM

CHEMISTRY INTERMEDIATE 1

Fill in these boxes and read what is printed below.

Full name of centre

Town

Forename(s)

Surname

Date of birth
Day Month Year Scottish candidate number Number of seat

Necessary data will be found in the Chemistry Data Booklet for Intermediate 1 and Access 3.

Section A   Questions 1 20 (20 marks)

Instructions for completion of **Section A** are given on page two.

For this section of the examination you must use an **HB pencil**.

Section B (40 marks)

All questions should be attempted.

The questions may be answered in any order but all answers are to be written in this answer book, **and must be written clearly and legibly in ink**.

Rough work, if any should be necessary, should be written in this book, and then scored through when the fair copy has been written. If further space is required, a supplementary sheet for rough work may be obtained from the Invigilator.

Additional space for answers will be found at the end of the book. If further space is required, supplementary sheets may be obtained from the Invigilator and should be inserted inside the **front** cover of this booklet.

Before leaving the examination room you must give this book to the Invigilator. If you do not, you may lose all the marks for this paper.

Read carefully

1. Check that the answer sheet provided is for **Chemistry Intermediate 1 (Section A)**.
2. For this section of the examination you must use an **HB pencil** and, where necessary, an eraser.
3. Check that the answer sheet you have been given has **your name**, **date of birth**, **SCN** (Scottish Candidate Number) and **Centre Name** printed on it.

   Do not change any of these details.
4. If any of this information is wrong, tell the Invigilator immediately.
5. If this information is correct, **print** your name and seat number in the boxes provided.
6. The answer to each question is **either** A, B, C or D. Decide what your answer is, then, using your pencil, put a horizontal line in the space provided (see sample question below).
7. There is **only one correct** answer to each question.
8. Any rough working should be done on the question paper or the rough working sheet, **not** on your answer sheet.
9. At the end of the examination, put the **answer sheet for Section A inside the front cover of this answer book**.

Sample Question

To show that the ink in a ball-pen consists of a mixture of dyes, the method of separation would be

A chromatography

B fractional distillation

C fractional crystallisation

D filtration.

The correct answer is **A**—chromatography. The answer **A** has been clearly marked in **pencil** with a horizontal line (see below).

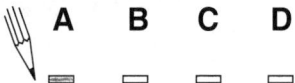

Changing an answer

If you decide to change your answer, carefully erase your first answer and using your pencil, fill in the answer you want. The answer below has been changed to **D**.

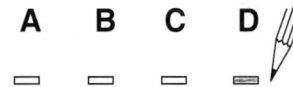

SECTION A

This section of the question paper consists of 20 multiple-choice questions.

1. Which of the following elements shows similar chemical properties to chlorine?

   (You may wish to use page 1 of the data booklet to help you.)

   A Argon
   B Iodine
   C Oxygen
   D Sulphur

2. Which of the following statements is true about a catalyst?

   A A catalyst is used up in a reaction.
   B A catalyst has no effect on a reaction.
   C A catalyst slows down a reaction.
   D A catalyst speeds up a reaction.

3. What is the formula for dinitrogen monoxide?

   A NO
   B NO_2
   C N_2O
   D N_2O_4

4. Which of the following is a common household alkali?

   A Soap
   B Vinegar
   C Lemonade
   D Soda water

5. Which of the following solutions is most acidic?

Solution	pH Value
A	8
B	7
C	4
D	2

6. A cell can be made using a lemon.

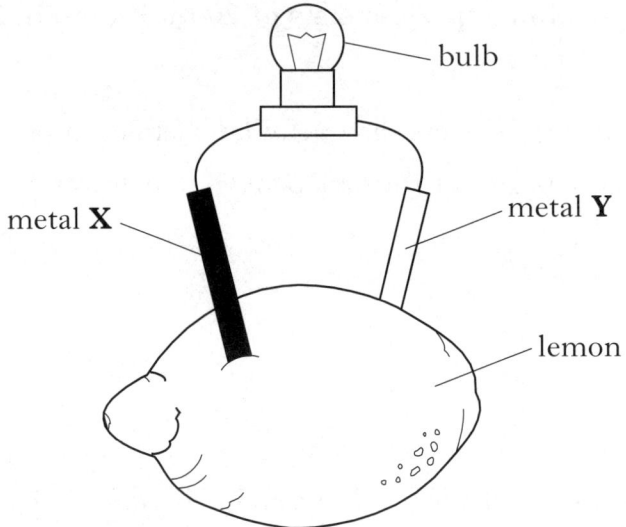

Which of the following pairs of metals would give the brightest bulb?

(You may wish to use page 6 of the data booklet to help you.)

	Metal X	Metal Y
A	magnesium	copper
B	copper	copper
C	zinc	copper
D	iron	copper

7. A detergent molecule can be shown as

When used in cleaning, the following happens.

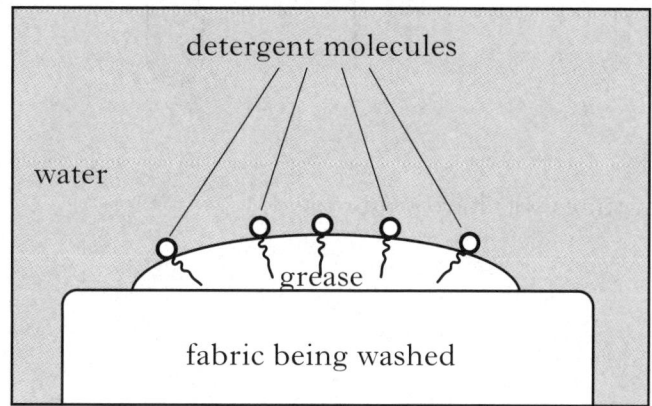

Which line in the table is true for the detergent to work?

	Head	Tail
A	soluble in grease	soluble in water
B	soluble in grease	soluble in grease
C	soluble in water	soluble in water
D	soluble in water	soluble in grease

[Turn over

8. A student shook different cleaning chemicals with water and the results are shown below.

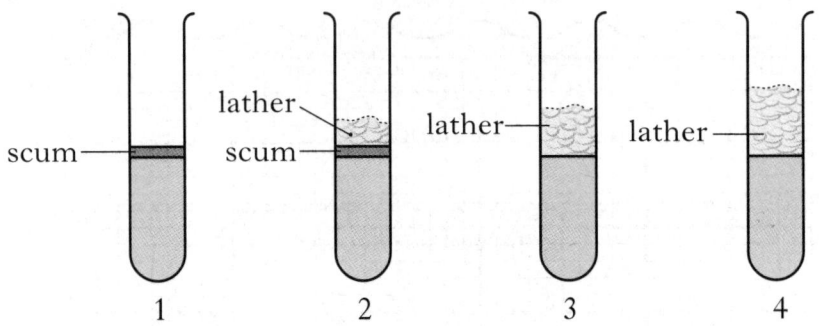

In which two test tubes was hard water used?

A 1 and 2
B 2 and 3
C 2 and 4
D 3 and 4

9.

The uniforms of firefighters need to be specially treated.

Which of the following two treatments would be most suitable?

A Dyeing and stain-proofing
B Flame-proofing and dyeing
C Stain-proofing and water-proofing
D Water-proofing and flame-proofing

10. Which fuel is made from sugar cane?

    A Biogas

    B Ethanol

    C Hydrogen

    D Petrol

11. When a sample of coal is burned the products include carbon dioxide and sulphur dioxide.

    From this information, which elements **must** be present in this sample of coal?

    A Carbon and oxygen

    B Carbon and sulphur

    C Sulphur and oxygen

    D Carbon, sulphur and oxygen

12. Uses of plastics are related to their properties.

    Which line in the table shows a plastic that could be used for covering electrical wires?

	Plastic	Property
A	PVC	flexible
B	Kevlar	very strong
C	Perspex	lets light through
D	Formica	high melting point

13. Which of the following properties is suitable for a plastic that is disposed of by burying?

    A Light

    B Thermoplastic

    C Biodegradable

    D Insoluble in water

14. Which process is described by the following word equation?

    carbon dioxide + water $\xrightarrow{\text{light}}$ glucose + oxygen

    A Fermentation

    B Photosynthesis

    C Polymerisation

    D Respiration

15. Which of the following statements is true?

  A Carbon dioxide in the air is **not** a cause of the greenhouse effect.

  B Clearing forests causes the carbon dioxide levels in the air to increase.

  C Burning petrol decreases carbon dioxide levels in the atmosphere.

  D Increasing levels of carbon dioxide in the air are causing the atmosphere to cool down.

16. Pesticides are used to

  A prevent bacteria and fungi causing disease

  B replace essential elements in the soil

  C prevent crops being eaten by insects

  D reduce the number of weeds.

17. The graph below can be used to determine weight conditions.

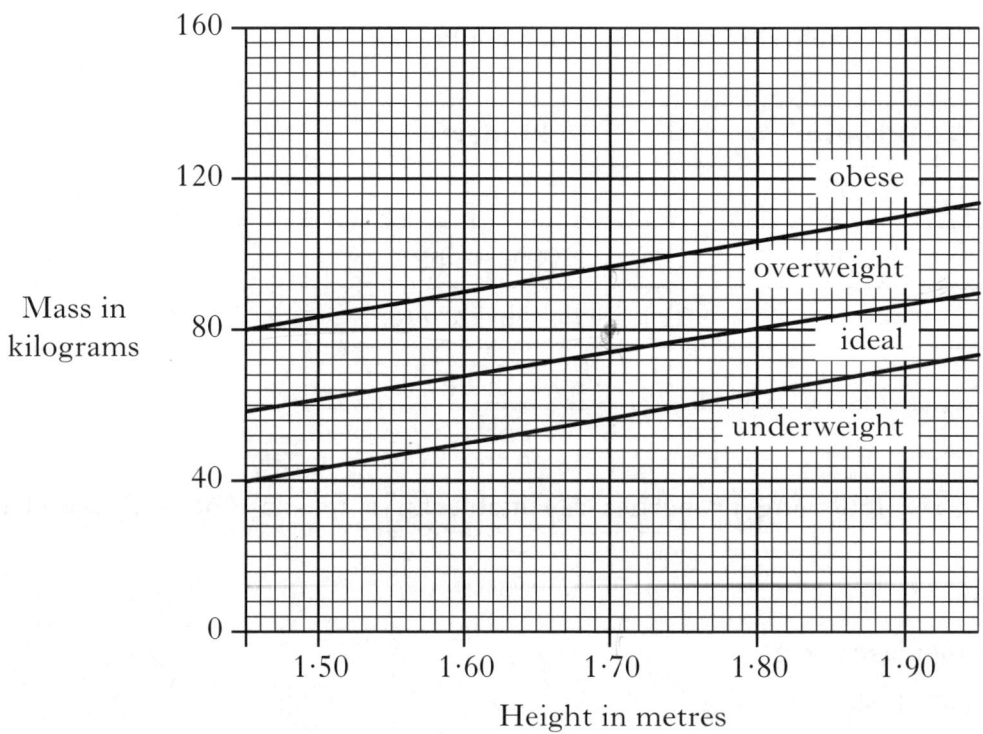

A man with a height of 1·70 metres weighs 80 kilograms.

Using the graph, how would he be described?

  A ideal

  B obese

  C overweight

  D underweight

18. Which of the following elements is required for healthy blood?

   A Iron
   B Copper
   C Calcium
   D Aluminium

19. The bar graph shows the number of drug-related deaths in Scotland over a six-year period.

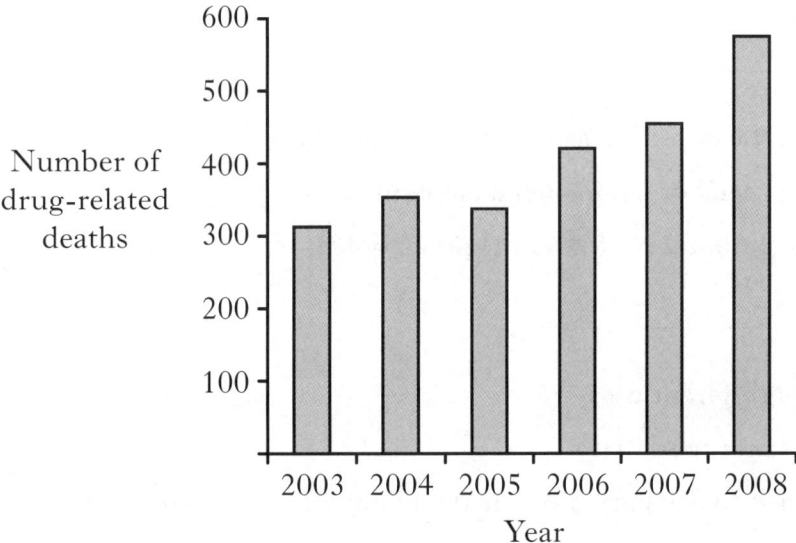

In general, over the six-year period, the bar graph shows that

   A there is no trend in the number of drug-related deaths
   B the number of drug-related deaths decreases
   C the number of drug-related deaths increases
   D the number of drug-related deaths stays constant.

20. Which of the following amounts of drink would the body break down in the shortest time?

   A 2 glasses of wine
   B 1 whisky
   C 1 bottle of alcopop
   D 1 pint of beer

Candidates are reminded that the answer sheet MUST be returned INSIDE this answer book.

[Turn over for Section B on *Page ten*

SECTION B

40 marks are available in this section of the paper.

All answers must be written clearly and legibly in ink.

1. Mercury is an element in the Periodic Table. It has an atomic number of 80.

    (a) Write the symbol for mercury.

    (You may wish to use page 8 of the data booklet to help you.)

    Hg

    (b) Elements can be classified as metals or non-metals.

    Is mercury a metal or a non-metal element?

    (You may with to use page 8 of the data booklet to help you.)

    metal

    (c) Mercury has different uses.

    State **one** use for mercury.

    (You may wish to use page 5 of the data booklet to help you.)

    Inside thermometers.

2. Sulphuric acid is an important chemical with many uses.

   (a) Sulphuric acid is corrosive.

   Circle the correct hazard symbol for sulphuric acid.

   (b) The table shows the percentages of sulphuric acid used to make different substances.

Use of sulphuric acid	Percentage (%) of sulphuric acid used
fertilisers	35
chemicals and detergents	30
paints	20
fibres	10
oil-refining	5

   (i) Complete the table to show percentage of sulphuric acid used in oil-refining.

   (ii) Use the information in the table to label the pie chart.

   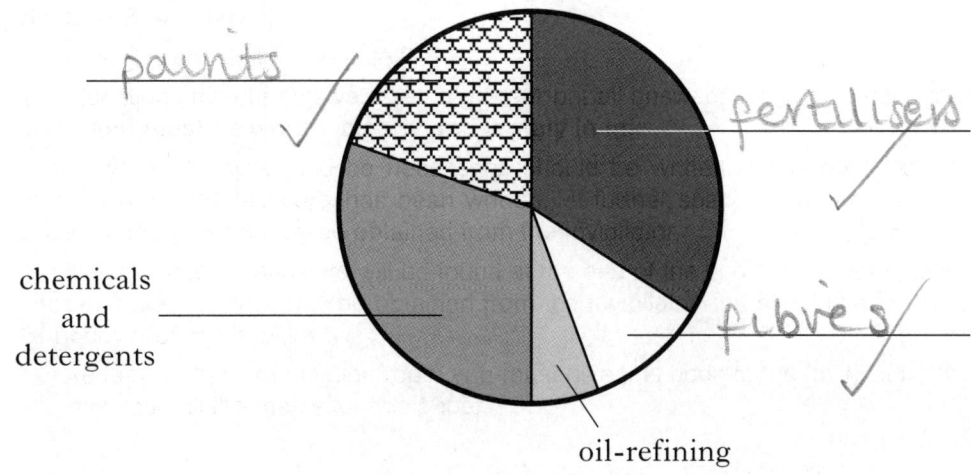

3. In the 1920s bicycle lamps were powered by burning acetylene gas.

A student made acetylene and burned it.

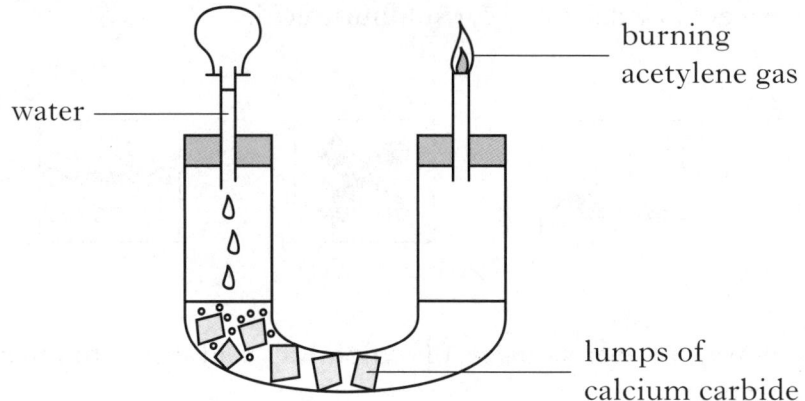

(a) How would the student know that a chemical reaction had taken place?

A new substance is formed. 1

(b) Calcium hydroxide solution is also produced when acetylene gas is made.

Complete the word equation for this reaction.

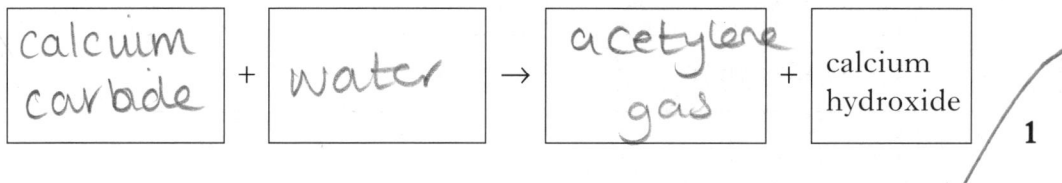

1

(c) The student repeated the experiment using **powdered** calcium carbide.

What would this do to the speed of the reaction?

It would react faster 1

(3)

4. Fish is a good source of protein in a healthy diet.

growth + repair.

(a) What are proteins used for in the body?

to build muscle. ✓

(b) When fish 'goes off' the smell is caused by the chemical trimethylamine.

The diagram below represents trimethylamine.

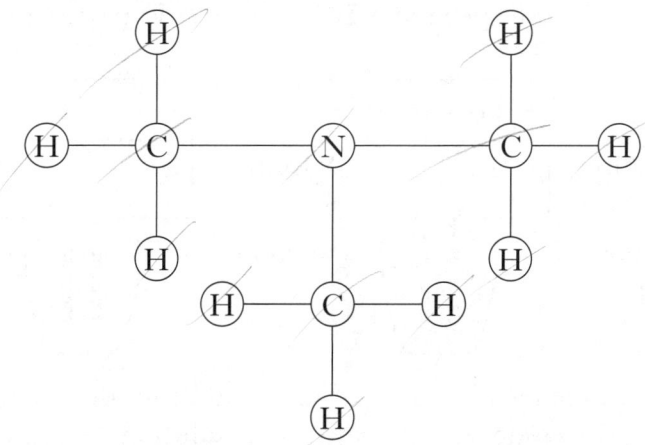

(i) Complete the formula to show the number of each type of atom in trimethylamine.

C _3_ H _9_ N _1_ ✓

(ii) Trimethylamine is made up of atoms held together by bonds.

What name is given to a group of atoms held together by bonds?

molecules. ✓

[Turn over

Marks

5. Lead bromide is a compound.

   (a) Name the elements in lead bromide.

   Pb, Br

   1

   (b) Lead bromide is an ionic compound made up of oppositely charged ions.

   Circle the correct words to complete the sentence.

   Ionic compounds tend to have {(high) / low} melting and boiling points as the bonds between the ions are {weak / (strong)}.

   1

   (c) A student carried out three experiments to investigate the conductivity of lead bromide.

   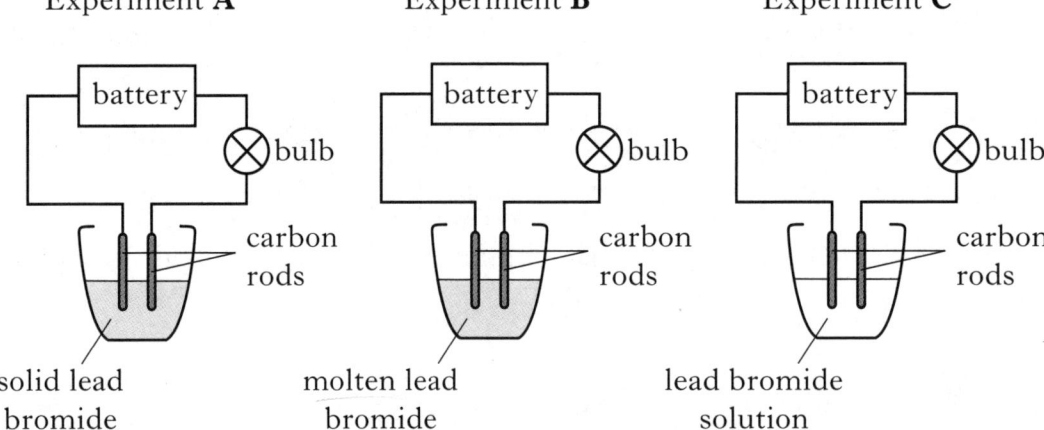

   Experiment **A** — solid lead bromide
   Experiment **B** — molten lead bromide
   Experiment **C** — lead bromide solution

   In which experiment will the bulb **not** light?

   Experiment A

   1

   (3)

6. A student added zinc to dilute hydrochloric acid.

   In this reaction, a zinc salt and hydrogen gas were formed.

   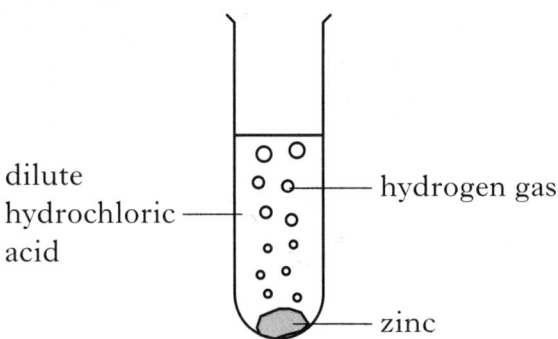

   (a) Complete the name of the salt formed in this reaction.

   zinc __chloride__

   (b) State the test for hydrogen gas.

   __It burns with a pop.__

   (c) The student repeated the experiment using metal **X**.

   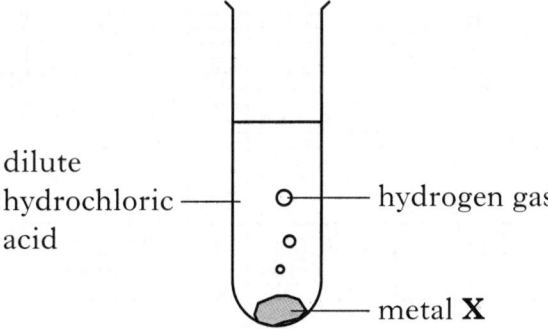

   She wrote the conclusion:

   "Metal **X** is less reactive than zinc."

   How did she know this?

   __As it only let off a few bubbles__

7. Some Euro coins are made from Nordic Gold, a mixture of copper, aluminium, zinc and tin.

(a) What term is used to describe a mixture of metals?

alloy

(b) The composition of Nordic Gold is shown in the table.

Metal	copper	aluminium	zinc	tin
Percentage (%)	88	6	4	2

Complete the bar graph to show the percentage of each metal in Nordic Gold.

(Additional graph paper, if required, can be found on *Page twenty-four*.)

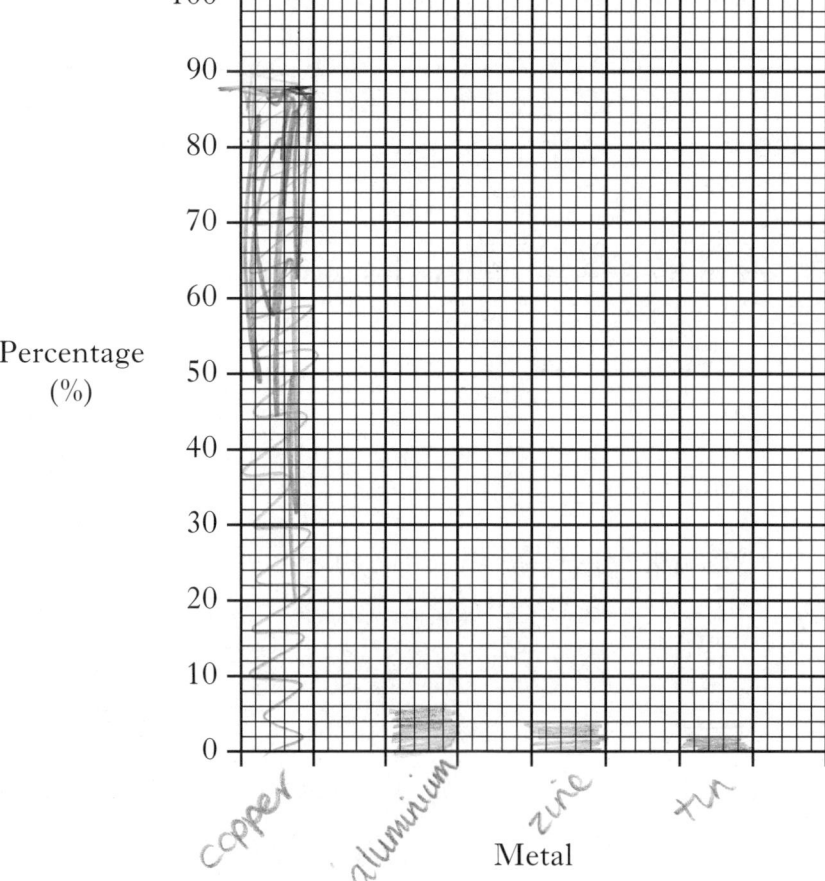

8. Rusting is the corrosion of iron.

(a) Water is needed for rusting to take place.

Name the other substance which **must** be present for iron to rust.

oxygen. ✓

(b) The following experiments were set up to find out if iron rusts when different metals are attached to it.

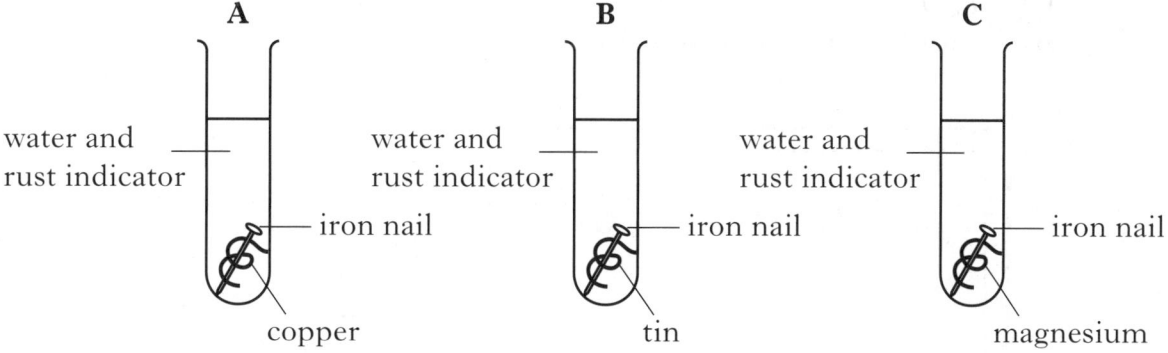

(i) What colour will the rust indicator turn to if the iron nail rusts?

blue. ✓

(ii) Circle the correct letter to complete the sentence.

(You may wish to use page 6 of the data booklet to help you.)

The iron nail in test-tube { A B **C** } will **not** rust. ✓

[Turn over

9. Coal is a fossil fuel.

    (a) Name another fossil fuel.

    peat

    (b) Coal was formed millions of years ago.

    What was coal made from?

    Plant and dead seacreature remains.

    (c) When coal is burned, carbon dioxide gas is produced.

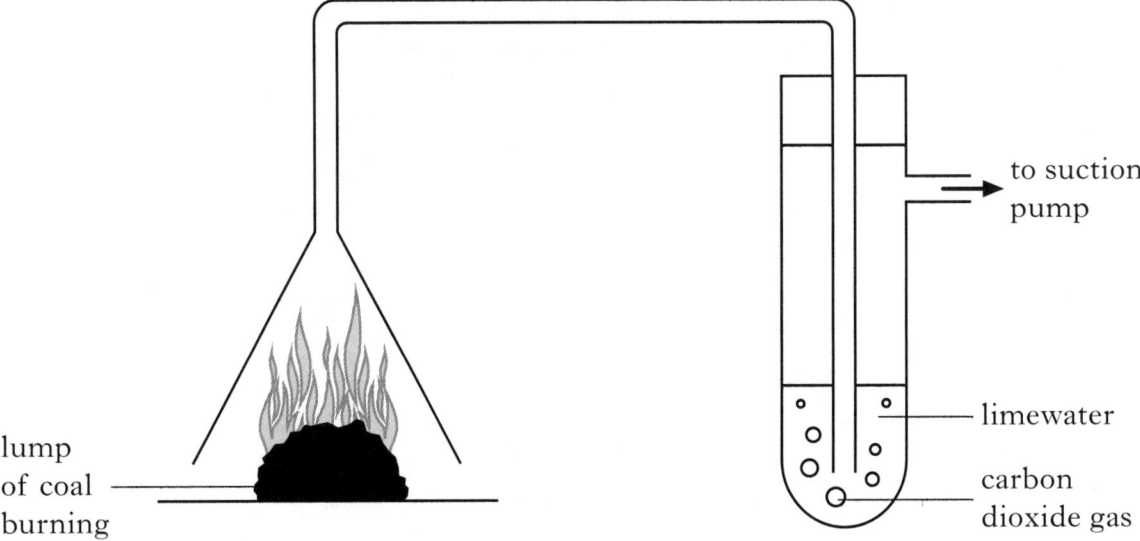

    What would you see happening when carbon dioxide is bubbled through limewater?

    turns limewater milky

10. This flow chart shows how a polymer is made.

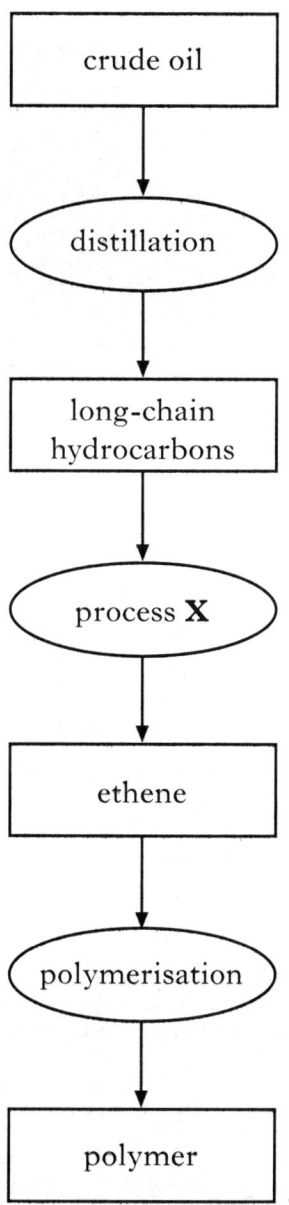

(a) Name process **X** which turns long-chain hydrocarbons into smaller, more useful ones like ethene.

cracking ✓

(b) Name the polymer formed from ethene.

polyethene ✓

(c) Many polymers are thermoplastic.
What is meant by thermoplastic?

It can be reshaped once heated. ✓

11. Fertilisers are added to soil to supply essential elements for healthy plant growth.

(a) Potassium and nitrogen are essential elements supplied by fertilisers.

Name another essential element.

Phosphorus ✓

(b) What **property** of potassium compounds makes them suitable for use as fertilisers?

(You may wish to use page 4 of the data booklet to help you.)

It is very soluble. ✓

(c) Peas are plants which have root nodules.

In root nodules, nitrogen from the air is converted to nitrates.

Name another plant which has root nodules.

Beans. ✓

12. In the **PPA**, "**Burning Carbohydrates**", the heat energy given out by burning different carbohydrates is compared.

The diagrams show 5 steps in this **PPA**.

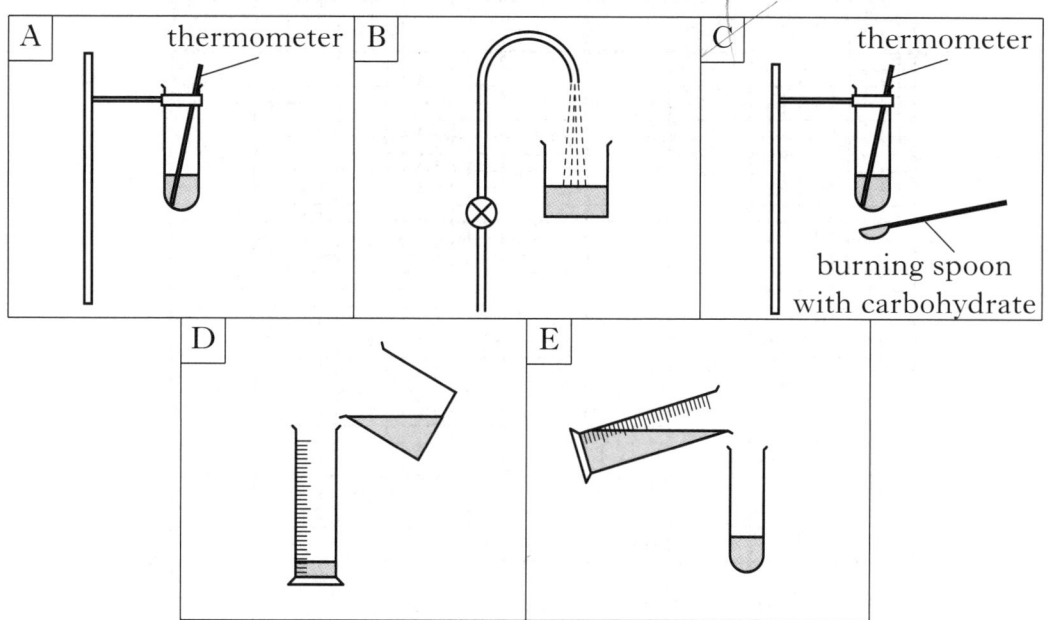

(a) Place a letter in each box to show the correct order in which the **PPA** is carried out.

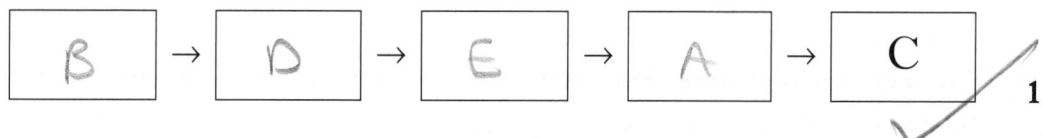

(b) The experiment was carried out using flour and then icing sugar.

The same volume of water was used each time.

State another factor which must be kept the same to make the experiment fair.

The same amount of flour

[Turn over

13. The following bar chart shows the nutritional content of a 100 g pizza.

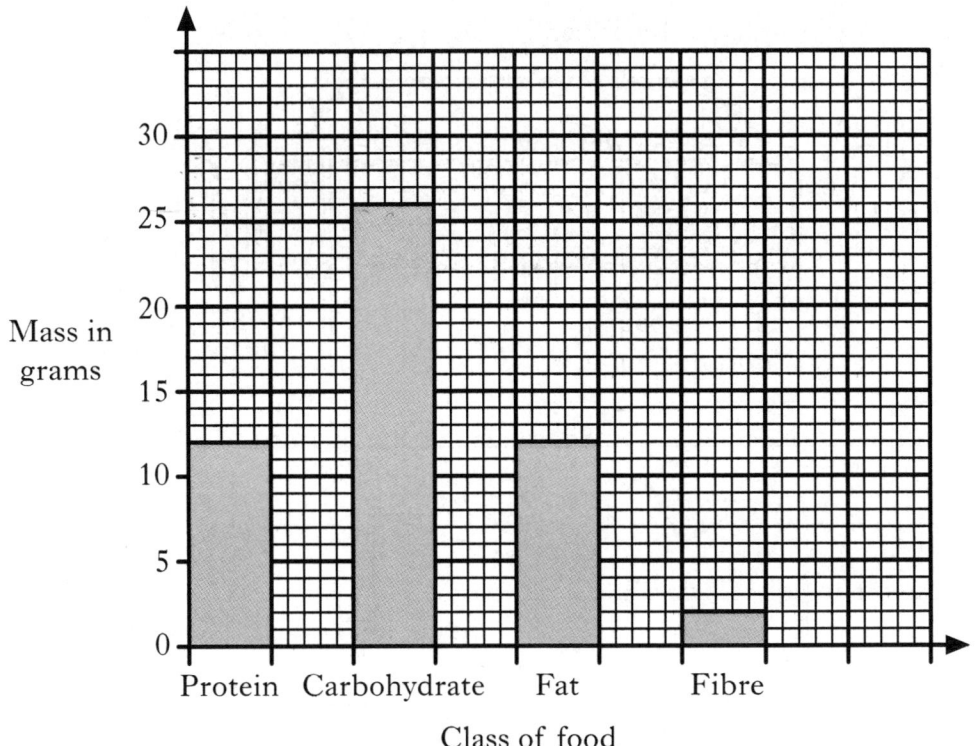

(a) What mass of carbohydrate is in this pizza?

___26___ grams

(b) The label on the pizza box shows that some of the carbohydrate was sugar.

Suggest a chemical name for the sugar present.

___glucose___

(c) Eating too much fat can result in high cholesterol in the blood stream. What health problem can this cause?

___heart attacks___

14. Medicines contain drugs which help the body when it is not working properly.

> **PAINEEZE**
>
> Contents:
>
> Ibuprofen
> Glycerol (E422)
> Manitol (E421)
> Saccharin solution (E954)

(a) (i) The E numbers shown on the contents are codes for food additives.

Why are additives used in medicines?

To taste nice. ✓

(ii) Ibuprofen is the active ingredient in Paineeze.

10 grams of Paineeze contains 1 gram of Ibuprofen.

Using the equation below, calculate the percentage of Ibuprofen in 10 grams of Paineeze.

$$\text{percentage Ibuprofen} = \frac{\text{mass of Ibuprofen}}{\text{mass of Paineeze}} \times 100$$

1 ÷ 10 = 0.1

0.1 × 100

10 ✓ %

(b) Micro-organisms interfere with chemical reactions which keep the body working properly.

What type of drug can be taken to fight micro-organisms?

Antibiotics ✓

[END OF QUESTION PAPER]

ADDITIONAL SPACE FOR ANSWERS

ADDITIONAL GRAPH PAPER FOR QUESTION 7(b).

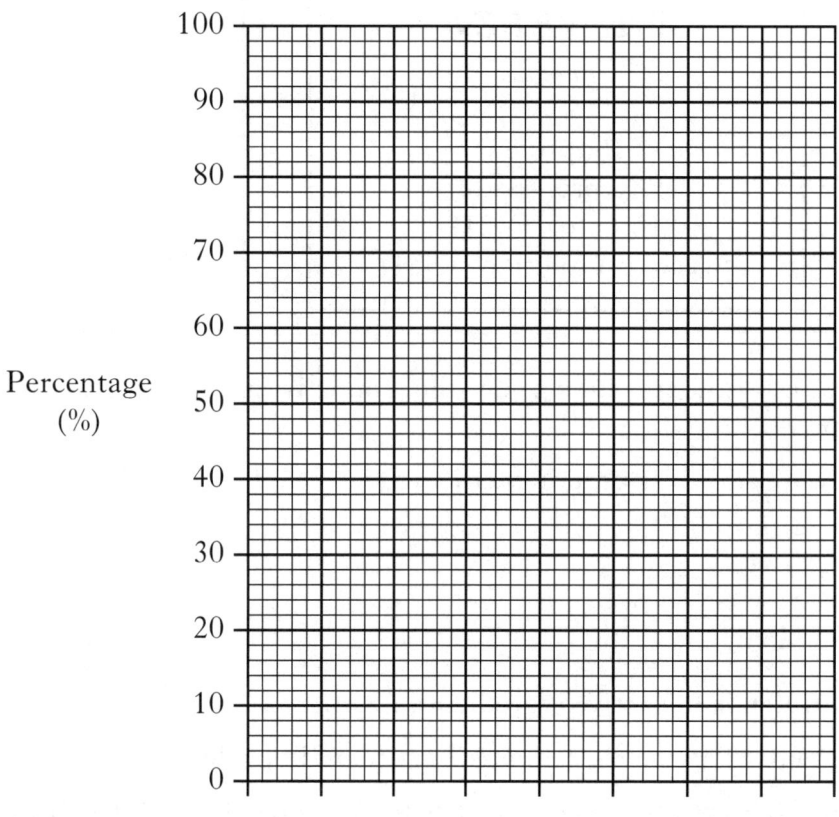

INTERMEDIATE 1
2011

FOR OFFICIAL USE

Section B   Total Marks

X012/101

NATIONAL QUALIFICATIONS 2011

THURSDAY, 26 MAY 1.00 PM – 2.30 PM

CHEMISTRY INTERMEDIATE 1

Fill in these boxes and read what is printed below.

Full name of centre

Town

Forename(s)

Surname

Date of birth
Day Month Year   Scottish candidate number   Number of seat

Necessary data will be found in the Chemistry Data Booklet for Intermediate 1 and Access 3.

Section A – Questions 1–20 (20 marks)

Instructions for completion of **Section A** are given on page two.

For this section of the examination you must use an **HB pencil**.

Section B (40 marks)

All questions should be attempted.

The questions may be answered in any order but all answers are to be written in this answer book, **and must be written clearly and legibly in ink**.

Rough work, if any should be necessary, should be written in this book, and then scored through when the fair copy has been written. If further space is required, a supplementary sheet for rough work may be obtained from the Invigilator.

Additional space for answers will be found at the end of the book. If further space is required, supplementary sheets may be obtained from the Invigilator and should be inserted inside the **front** cover of this booklet.

Before leaving the examination room you must give this book to the Invigilator. If you do not, you may lose all the marks for this paper.

Read carefully

1. Check that the answer sheet provided is for **Chemistry Intermediate 1 (Section A)**.
2. For this section of the examination you must use an **HB pencil** and, where necessary, an eraser.
3. Check that the answer sheet you have been given has **your name**, **date of birth**, **SCN** (Scottish Candidate Number) and **Centre Name** printed on it.
   Do not change any of these details.
4. If any of this information is wrong, tell the Invigilator immediately.
5. If this information is correct, **print** your name and seat number in the boxes provided.
6. The answer to each question is **either** A, B, C or D. Decide what your answer is, then, using your pencil, put a horizontal line in the space provided (see sample question below).
7. There is **only one correct** answer to each question.
8. Any rough working should be done on the question paper or the rough working sheet, **not** on your answer sheet.
9. At the end of the examination, put the **answer sheet for Section A inside the front cover of this answer book**.

Sample Question

To show that the ink in a ball-pen consists of a mixture of dyes, the method of separation would be

A chromatography

B fractional distillation

C fractional crystallisation

D filtration.

The correct answer is **A**—chromatography. The answer **A** has been clearly marked in **pencil** with a horizontal line (see below).

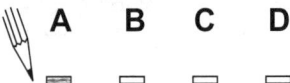

Changing an answer

If you decide to change your answer, carefully erase your first answer and using your pencil, fill in the answer you want. The answer below has been changed to **D**.

SECTION A

This section of the question paper consists of 20 multiple-choice questions.

1. Which hazard does the following symbol indicate?

   - A Corrosive
   - B Flammable
   - C Irritant
   - D Toxic

2. The structures of substances can be represented by models.

   Which model shows a **compound** made of molecules?

   A

   B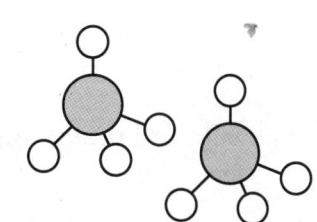

   C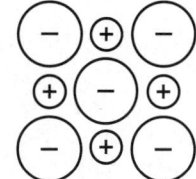

   D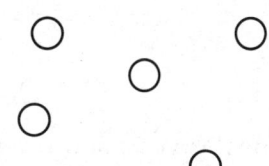

3. When water changes to steam
   - A strong bonds between atoms in water molecules are broken
   - B strong bonds between water molecules are broken
   - C weak bonds between atoms in water molecules are broken
   - D weak bonds between water molecules are broken.

4. As water is added to an acid, the acid becomes

A more acidic and its pH goes down

B more acidic and its pH goes up

C less acidic and its pH goes up

D less acidic and its pH goes down.

5. sodium hydroxide + sulphuric acid ⟶ salt + water

The name of the salt produced in this reaction is

A hydrogen sulphate

B hydrogen sulphide

C sodium sulphate

D sodium sulphide.

6. Which of the following elements is a conductor of electricity?

A Aluminium

B Iodine

C Silicon

D Sulphur

7. Which of the following metals is found uncombined in the Earth's crust?

A Magnesium

B Sodium

C Gold

D Iron

8. Which type of cleaning chemical gives a scum with hard water?

A Soap

B Shampoo

C Washing-up liquid

D Soapless detergent

9. Cleaning chemicals remove oil and grease stains from clothes by

   A cracking the oil and grease

   B boiling off the oil and grease

   C neutralising the oil and grease

   D breaking up the oil and grease into tiny droplets.

10. Which of the following fibres is made by the chemical industry?

   A Cotton

   B Nylon

   C Silk

   D Wool

11. Which line in the table shows properties of a plastic which could be suitable for use in greenhouses instead of glass?

	Lets light through	Effect of heat	Effect of light
A	yes	none	becomes brittle
B	no	none	none
C	yes	none	very little
D	yes	cracks	very little

12. Plastics are said to be biodegradable if they are broken down by

   A bacteria in the soil

   B acid in the soil

   C plants in the soil

   D water in the soil.

13. Which of the following gases is toxic and can be produced when plastics burn?

   A Nitrogen

   B Water vapour

   C Carbon monoxide

   D Carbon dioxide

[Turn over

14. Which of the following compounds could be used as a fertiliser?

    (You may wish to use page 4 of the data booklet to help you.)

    A   Calcium carbonate
    B   Potassium phosphate
    C   Magnesium chloride
    D   Iron sulphate

15. Which of the following foods contains more fat than carbohydrate?

    (You may wish to use page 7 of the data booklet to help you.)

    A   Bread
    B   Peanuts
    C   Rice
    D   Spaghetti

16. What percentage of body weight is water?

    A   less than 40%
    B   between 40% and 50%
    C   between 50% and 60%
    D   more than 60%

17. Which of the following compounds can be used to break down starch?

    A   Acid
    B   Alcohol
    C   Fat
    D   Sugar

18. Which of the following statements about fibre in the diet is **not** true?

    A   It keeps the gut working well.
    B   It absorbs water and swells.
    C   It prevents constipation.
    D   It supplies vitamins.

19. Alcohol is made by the fermentation of glucose.

    Distillation can then be used to

    A   increase the glucose concentration

    B   decrease the alcohol concentration

    C   increase the alcohol concentration

    D   decrease the glucose concentration.

20. Which of the following drugs can fight micro-organisms?

    A   Antibiotics

    B   Caffeine

    C   Nicotine

    D   Alcohol

Candidates are reminded that the answer sheet MUST be returned INSIDE this answer book.

[*Turn over for Section B on Page eight*

SECTION B

40 marks are available in this section of the paper.

All answers must be written clearly and legibly in ink.

1. Chlorine, fluorine and argon are the names of elements found in the Periodic Table.

    (a) Are they metals or non-metals?

    (You may wish to use page 1 of the data booklet to help you.)

    non metals ✓   **1**

    (b) Argon is found in column 0 of the Periodic Table.

    Name an element which has similar chemical properties to Argon.

    Neon. ✓   **1**

    (c) Fluorine is used to make sodium fluoride which is added to drinking water.

    Why is sodium fluoride added to drinking water?

    prevent tooth decay ✓   **1**

    (3)

2. A student carried out an investigation using three catalysts; zinc oxide, copper oxide and manganese oxide.

(a) What is the purpose of a catalyst?

Speed up a chemical reaction

(b) The student added 2 grams of each powdered catalyst into a measuring cylinder containing 20 cm³ of hydrogen peroxide and detergent. A lather was produced which rose up the measuring cylinder. After 30 seconds, the volume of lather was measured.

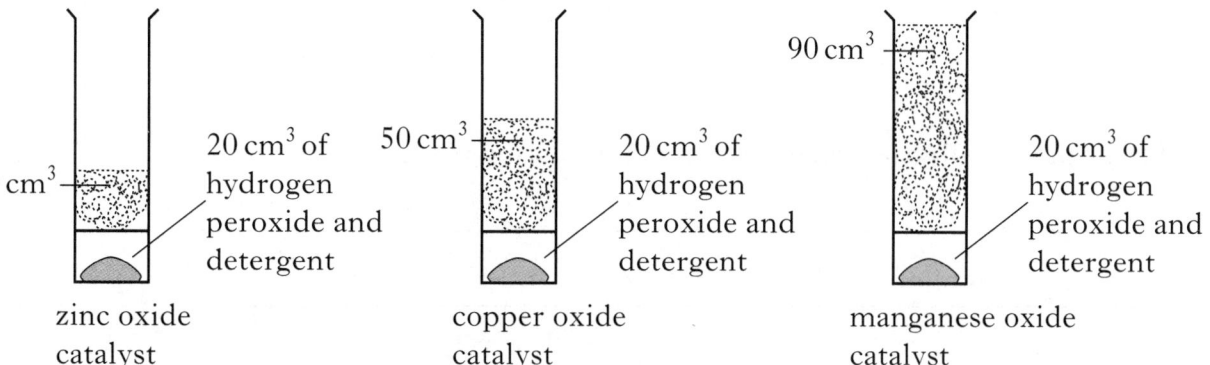

(i) Which catalyst worked best on the reaction?

manganese oxide catalyst

(ii) State **two ways** in which the student made sure the investigation was fair.

1 *same amount of compound*

2 *same amount of solution*

(iii) The lather formed as oxygen gas was produced.

What is the test for oxygen gas?

relights a glowing splint

[Turn over

3. In vineyards, strips of copper are covered with the skins of fermented grapes. The brown copper reacts with chemicals from the grape skins to form green copper ethanoate, which is known as verdigris.

(a) How can you tell that a chemical reaction has taken place?

A new substance has been formed **1**

(b) Copper ethanoate contains copper, carbon and hydrogen.

The ending –ate indicates that another element is also present in this compound.

Name this element.

oxygen **1**

(c) A solution of copper ethanoate can be sprayed on plants as a fungicide.

What is a fungicide?

Stops diseases **1**

(3)

4. A student carried out an experiment to find the pH values of different garden soils.

Water was slowly poured through a sample of soil and a solution was collected.

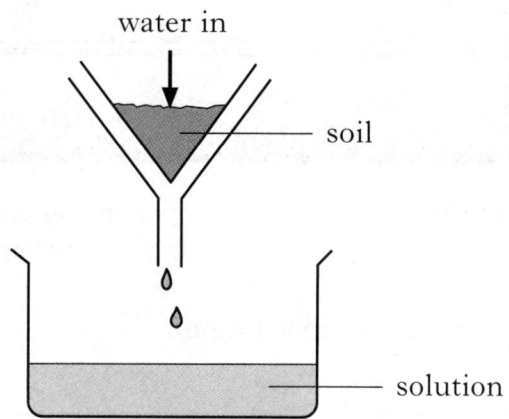

(a) How would the student find out the pH of the solution using pH paper and a colour chart?

By matching the colars up to find out if it is an acid or alkali

(b) The pH values of the garden soils are shown.

Garden	pH of soil
A	5·0
B	6·5
C	7·0
D	8·0
E	9·5

(i) Which garden has the most alkaline soil?

Garden ___E___

(ii) (Circle) the correct word to complete the sentence.

The pH of soil in garden B can be increased by adding { acid / salt / **alkali** / alcohol }.

5. (a) Some calculators use batteries which contain the chemicals zinc and silver oxide.

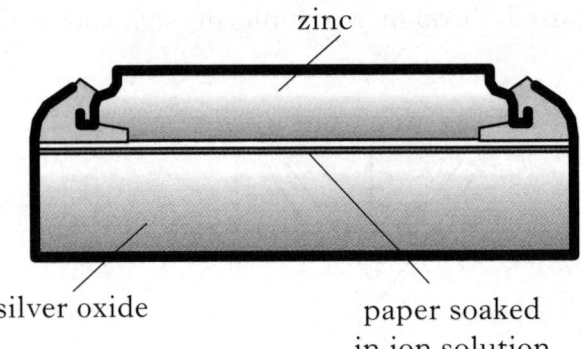

What is the purpose of the ion solution?

So it reacts. **1**

(b) A student made a battery from a lemon and two strips of metal. The voltage produced was measured.

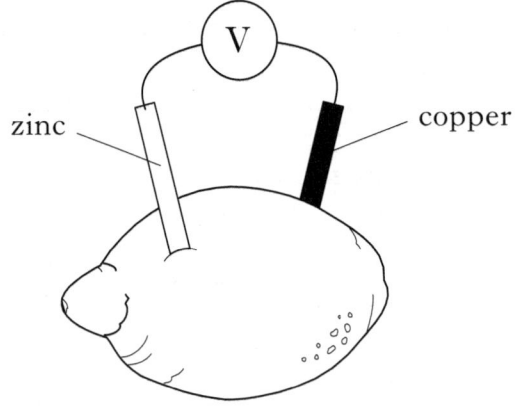

Voltage produced = 1·1 V

The student changed the strip of zinc to a strip of magnesium.

How would the voltage of the lemon battery change?

(You may wish to use page 6 of the data booklet to help you.)

It would increase **1**

(c) Batteries eventually stop working.

Why does this happen?

The chemical runs out **1**

(3)

6. A car has been developed that is fuelled by hydrogen. Hydrogen is being marketed as an alternative to petrol as it is a clean source of energy.

(a) **Water** is formed when **hydrogen** burns in **oxygen**.

Write a word equation for this reaction.

| hydrogen | + | oxygen | → | water |

(b) State **one** safety concern when using hydrogen gas as an alternative fuel to petrol.

It can explode

(c) Using the following information and formula, calculate the distance a hydrogen-fuelled car can travel on a full fuel tank.

INFORMATION
Fuel consumption = 2·5 miles per litre
Fuel tank capacity = 50 litres

Distance travelled = **fuel consumption** × **fuel tank capacity**

= 2·5 × 50

= 125 miles

[Turn over

7. Metal spectacle frames have plastic side tips.

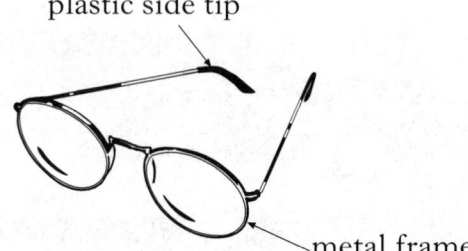

(a) The frame is made from "German silver", which is a mixture of three metals.

(i) What name is given to a mixture of metals?

An alloy.

(ii) The table gives information about the percentage of each metal in "German silver".

Metal in German silver	Percentage (%)
copper	60
nickel	15
zinc	25

Use this information to label the pie chart.

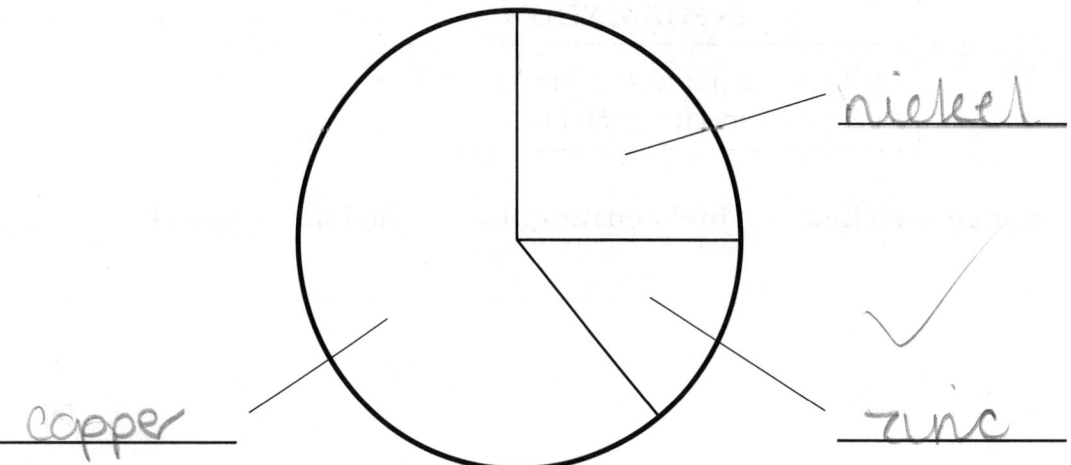

(b) In order to make the spectacle frame fit around the ear, the plastic side tips are reshaped after heating.

What name is given to this type of plastic?

Thermoplastic

Marks

8. (a) Peat is found in many parts of Scotland. It is an example of a fossil fuel.

(i) What is peat made from?

plants ✓   **1**

(ii) Some countries, such as Finland, burn peat in power stations to provide energy.

There is concern about using peat in this way as it is a finite resource.

What is meant by a finite resource?

It will run out. ✓   **1**

(b) Information about some fuels is shown in the tables.

Number of carbon atoms	Energy released in kilojoules
1	891
2	1560
3	2220
4	2877

Name of fuel	Number of carbon atoms
methane	1
ethane	2
propane	3
butane	4

(i) Complete the sentence.

As the number of carbon atoms increases, the energy released _increases_. ✓   **1**

(ii) Name the fuel which releases 1560 kilojoules of energy.

ethane ✓   **1**

(4)

9. The following is an extract from a poem which won the Royal Society of Chemistry Bill Bryson prize for science communication.

> Once upon a time the world was sad
> Its atmosphere was feeling bad
> There was too much CO_2
> (Carbon dioxide to me and you)
> It made it hotter and hotter still
> And all the fishes it did kill
>   Rachel Farnsworth

(a) An increase in the level of carbon dioxide causes the atmosphere to retain more of the sun's energy as heat.

Name this process.

Greenhouse effect

(b) State **one** reason why the level of carbon dioxide in the atmosphere has increased.

increase of cars

(c) Plants use up carbon dioxide and water in photosynthesis.

Complete the labelled diagram to show what is made in this process.

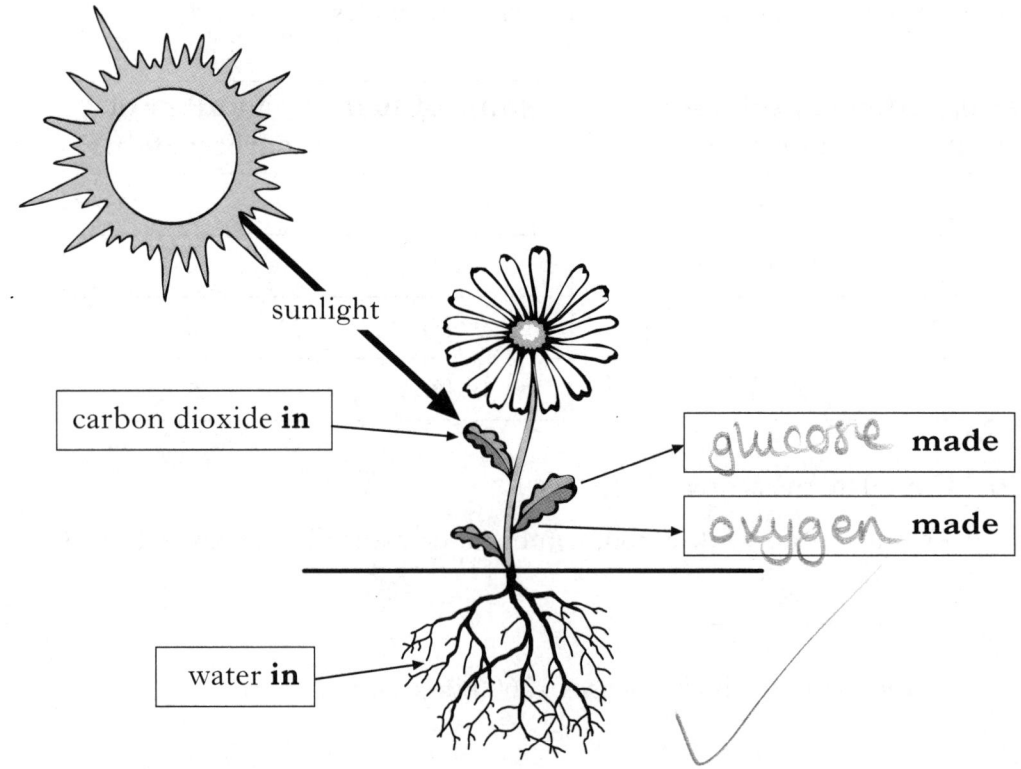

glucose **made**

oxygen **made**

[Turn over for Question 10 on *Page eighteen*

10. Treacle tart is a popular dessert.

The pastry case is made using butter and the filling is made using breadcrumbs and syrup.

(a) Butter is a fat.

(i) What does fat provide in our diet?

energy

(ii) Fats can be described as saturated.

What effect do saturated fats have on cholesterol levels in the blood?

It increases cholesterol levels.

(b) What indicator could be used to show that breadcrumbs contain starch?

Benedicts solution

10. (continued)

(c) A student carried out an investigation to show how temperature affects the speed of the reaction between a sugar, found in syrup, and Benedict's solution.

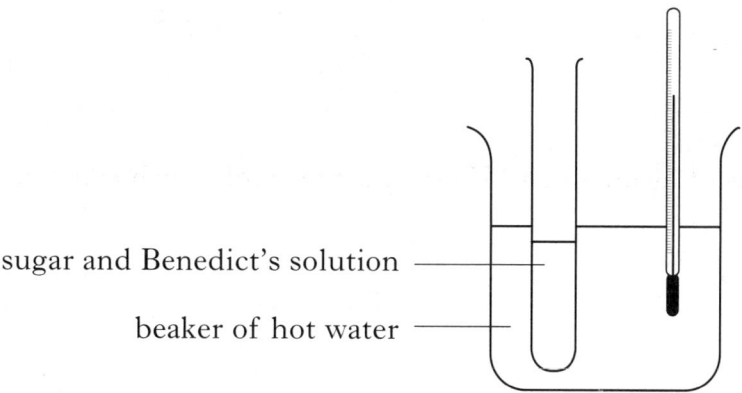

sugar and Benedict's solution
beaker of hot water

The results are shown.

Temperature of water in °C	Time for reaction to take place in seconds
50	118
60	64
70	37
80	18

(i) How does increasing the temperature affect the speed of the reaction?

It speeds it up. 1

(ii) Predict how long the reaction would take at 65 °C.

___10___ seconds 1

(iii) The Benedict's solution changed colour showing that a reaction had taken place.

The colour change was _blue_ to _black_. 1

(6)

[Turn over

11. (a) The government publishes guidelines on the recommended maximum units of alcohol that can be drunk in one day.

The units of alcohol can be calculated using the formula:

$$\text{units of alcohol} = \frac{\text{volume in cm}^3 \times \text{percentage alcohol (\%)}}{1000}$$

Calculate the units of alcohol in a 175 cm³ glass of wine which contains 12% alcohol.

175 × 12 = 2100

2100 ÷ 1000 = 2.1

_____2_____ units   1

(b) A man drank a pint of beer containing 3 units of alcohol.

How long will it take for his body to break down the alcohol?

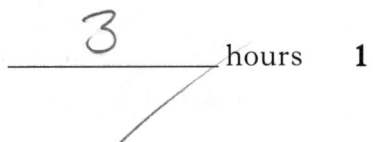

_____3_____ hours   1

11. (continued)

(c) The table gives information on the alcohol content of some beers.

Beer	Alcohol by volume (%)
Hawley's Best	3·8
Spier's Special	5·4
Dobson's Delight	6·2
Munro's Magic	7·6

Draw a bar graph to show this information.

(Additional graph paper, if required, can be found on *Page twenty-two*.)

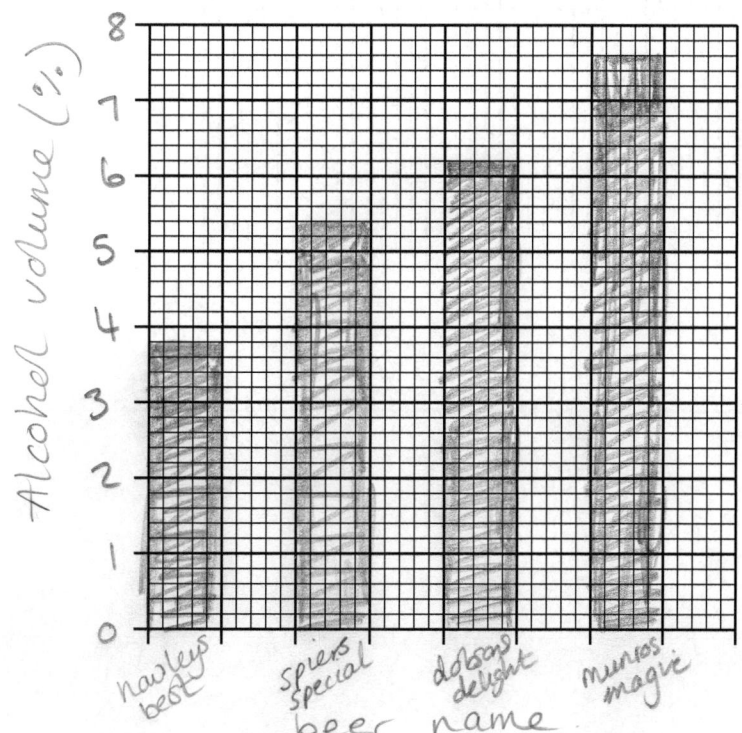

(d) Preservatives, added to beers to improve the keeping qualities, are examples of food additives.

Give another **use** of food additives.

help them taste better

[END OF QUESTION PAPER]

ADDITIONAL SPACE FOR ANSWERS

ADDITIONAL GRAPH PAPER FOR QUESTION 11(c).

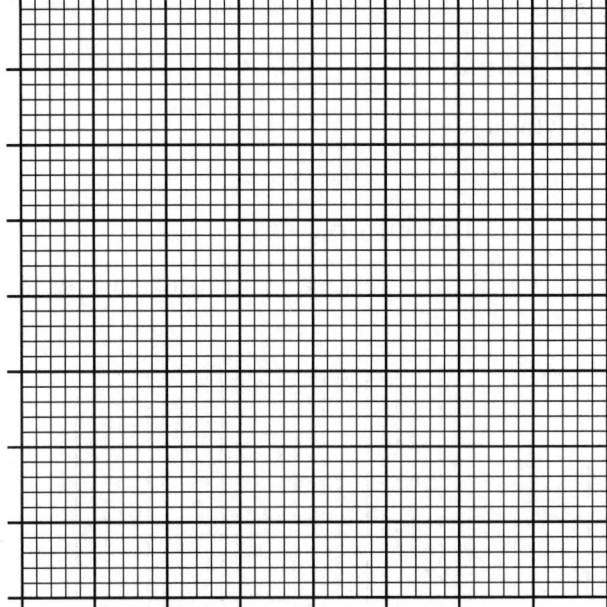

ADDITIONAL SPACE FOR ANSWERS

INTERMEDIATE 1
2012

OFFICIAL SQA PAST PAPERS   115   INTERMEDIATE 1 CHEMISTRY 2012

FOR OFFICIAL USE

Section B   Total Marks

X012/10/02

NATIONAL QUALIFICATIONS 2012
MONDAY, 14 MAY 1.00 PM – 2.30 PM

CHEMISTRY INTERMEDIATE 1

Fill in these boxes and read what is printed below.

Full name of centre

Town

Forename(s)

Surname

Date of birth
Day   Month   Year   Scottish candidate number   Number of seat

Necessary data will be found in the Chemistry Data Booklet for Intermediate 1 and Access 3.

Section A – Questions 1–20 (20 marks)

Instructions for completion of **Section A** are given on page two.

For this section of the examination you must use an **HB pencil**.

Section B (40 marks)

All questions should be attempted.

The questions may be answered in any order but all answers are to be written in this answer book, **and must be written clearly and legibly in ink**.

Rough work, if any should be necessary, should be written in this book, and then scored through when the fair copy has been written. If further space is required, a supplementary sheet for rough work may be obtained from the Invigilator.

Additional space for answers will be found at the end of the book. If further space is required, supplementary sheets may be obtained from the Invigilator and should be inserted inside the **front** cover of this booklet.

Before leaving the examination room you must give this book to the Invigilator. If you do not, you may lose all the marks for this paper.

SA X012/10/02 6/6510

Read carefully

1. Check that the answer sheet provided is for **Chemistry Intermediate 1 (Section A)**.
2. For this section of the examination you must use an **HB pencil** and, where necessary, an eraser.
3. Check that the answer sheet you have been given has **your name, date of birth, SCN** (Scottish Candidate Number) and **Centre Name** printed on it.

   Do not change any of these details.
4. If any of this information is wrong, tell the Invigilator immediately.
5. If this information is correct, **print** your name and seat number in the boxes provided.
6. The answer to each question is **either** A, B, C or D. Decide what your answer is, then, using your pencil, put a horizontal line in the space provided (see sample question below).
7. There is **only one correct** answer to each question.
8. Any rough working should be done on the question paper or the rough working sheet, **not** on your answer sheet.
9. At the end of the examination, put the **answer sheet for Section A inside the front cover of this answer book**.

Sample Question

To show that the ink in a ball-pen consists of a mixture of dyes, the method of separation would be

A chromatography

B fractional distillation

C fractional crystallisation

D filtration.

The correct answer is **A**—chromatography. The answer **A** has been clearly marked in **pencil** with a horizontal line (see below).

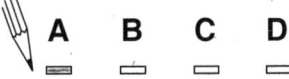

Changing an answer

If you decide to change your answer, carefully erase your first answer and using your pencil, fill in the answer you want. The answer below has been changed to **D**.

SECTION A

This section of the question paper consists of 20 multiple-choice questions.

1. Which of the following **always** occurs when a chemical reaction takes place?

   A   A gas is produced.
   B   A precipitate is formed.
   C   A colour change takes place.
   D   A new substance is formed.

2. Which line in the table correctly describes what happens if 1 gram of a catalyst is involved in a chemical reaction?

	Speed of reaction	Mass of catalyst left at end in grams
A	faster	1
B	unchanged	1
C	faster	0
D	unchanged	0

3. The diagram below shows a water molecule.

   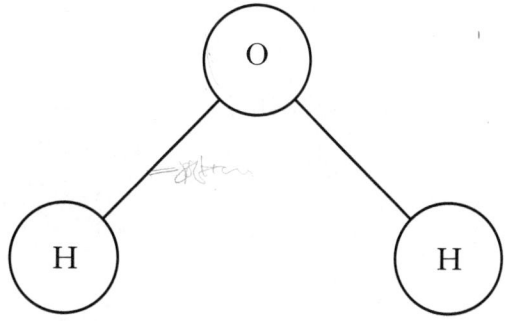

   Which of the following statements correctly describes this molecule?

   A   Atoms held together by weak bonds
   B   Atoms held together by strong bonds
   C   Ions held together by weak bonds
   D   Ions held together by strong bonds

[Turn over

4. The table shows information about four compounds.

Compound	Solubility in water	Conductivity when molten
1	soluble	conducts
2	soluble	does not conduct
3	insoluble	conducts
4	insoluble	does not conduct

Which of the following statements is correct?

A   Compounds **1** and **2** are ionic.

B   Compounds **3** and **4** are ionic.

C   Compounds **1** and **3** are ionic.

D   Compounds **2** and **4** are ionic.

5. The formula for dinitrogen tetroxide is

A N_2O_3

B N_2O

C NO_2

D N_2O_4.

6. The pH of a solution can be measured using

A   Benedict's solution

B   Universal indicator

C   iodine solution

D   limewater.

7. A student shook samples of hard water with different cleaning chemicals. The results are shown below.

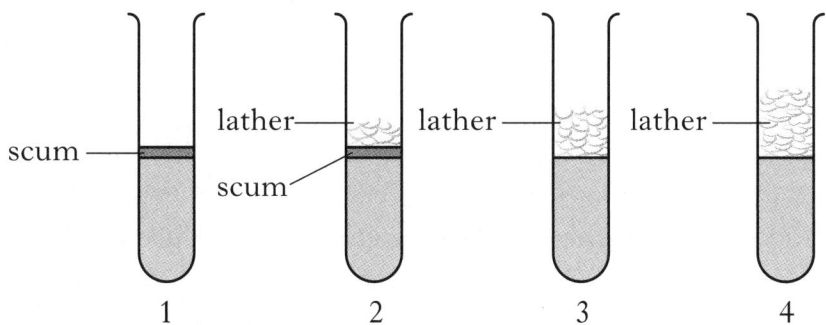

In which **two** test tubes was soapless detergent used?

A 1 and 2
B 2 and 3
C 3 and 4
D 1 and 4

8. Cleaning chemicals remove oil and grease stains from clothes by

A cracking the oil and grease
B boiling off the oil and grease
C neutralising the oil and grease
D breaking the oil and grease into tiny droplets.

9. Which of the following contain only **natural** fibres?

A Cotton and silk
B Polyester and silk
C Cotton and nylon
D Polyester and nylon

10. For safety reasons, fabrics used to make nightdresses are specially treated. This type of treatment makes the nightdresses

A stain proof
B flameproof
C waterproof
D hard wearing.

11. In which of the following reactions is oxygen used up?

    A Combustion
    B Neutralisation
    C Photosynthesis
    D Polymerisation

12. Which **two** substances react together inside a car engine to produce a poisonous gas?

    A Hydrogen and oxygen
    B Hydrogen and water
    C Nitrogen and water
    D Nitrogen and oxygen

13. Which of the following substances is a monomer?

    A Styrene
    B Perspex
    C Kevlar
    D Bakelite

14. The triangle shows that a fuel, oxygen and heat are needed for a fire.

    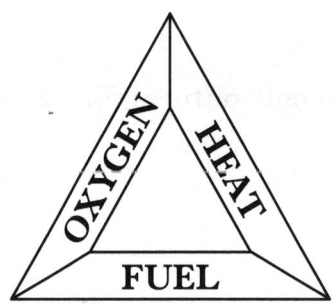

    Spraying water on a bonfire puts out the fire by

    A soaking up the fuel
    B preventing oxygen getting to the fuel
    C lowering the temperature of the fuel
    D providing carbon dioxide to put out the fire.

15. Which statement about pesticides is **false**?

A They are toxic.
B They kill weeds.
C They control pests.
D They improve crop yield.

16. Which of the following plants do **not** have root nodules?

A Beans
B Carrots
C Clover
D Peas

17.

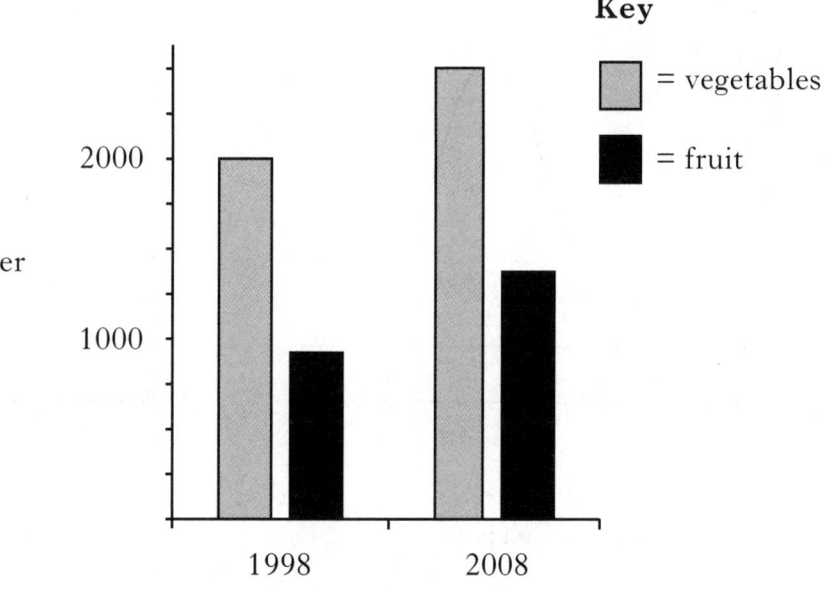

Compared with 1998, in 2008 people ate

A less vegetables and less fruit
B less vegetables and more fruit
C more vegetables and less fruit
D more vegetables and more fruit.

[**Turn over**

18. When food is digested in the body, proteins are broken down by enzymes.

Which graph shows that the enzymes work fastest at 37 °C?

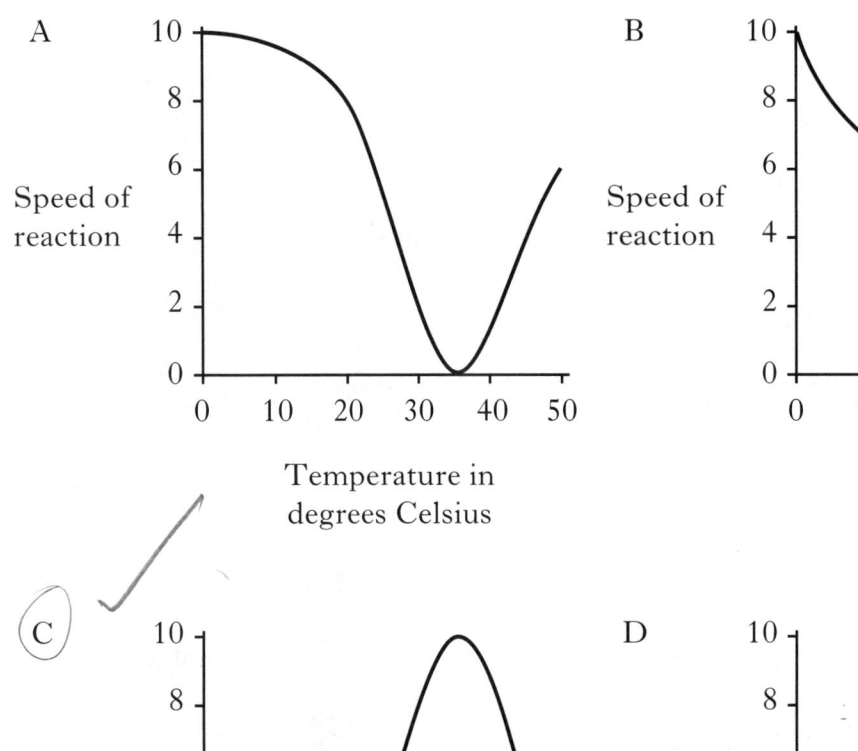

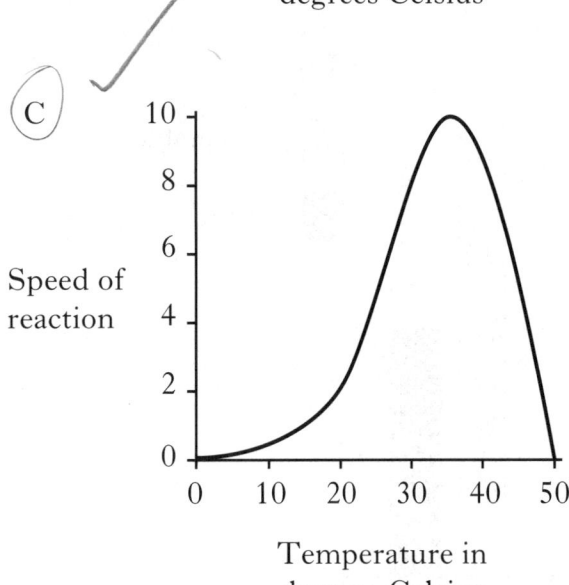
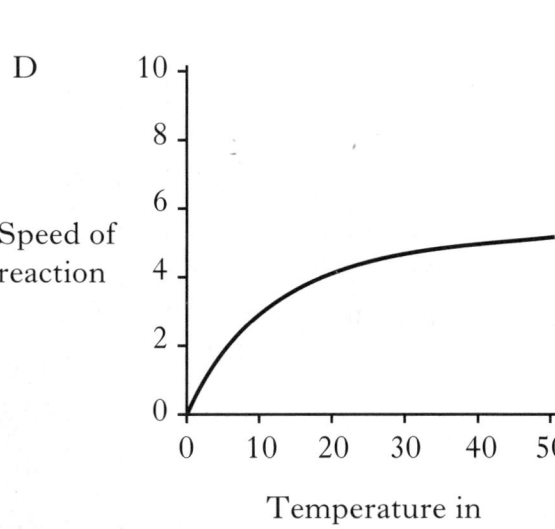

19. Which drink is made by fermentation followed by distillation?

- A Beer (5% alcohol)
- B Cider (8% alcohol)
- C Rum (40% alcohol)
- D Wine (11% alcohol)

20. Which statement about all drugs is correct?

A They alter the way in which the body works.
B They can damage health.
C They can help the body.
D They are illegal.

Candidates are reminded that the answer sheet MUST be returned INSIDE this answer book.

[*Turn over for Section B on Page ten*

SECTION B

40 marks are available in this section of the paper.

All answers must be written clearly and legibly in ink.

1. Fireworks contain many different chemicals.

   (a) Lithium carbonate is commonly used to give a red colour to fireworks.

   Complete the sentence.

   Lithium carbonate contains the elements ___lithium___, ___carbon___ and ___oxygen___.

   (b) Magnesium is added to fireworks as it produces a very bright white light when it reacts with oxygen. Magnesium oxide is made in this reaction.

   Complete the word equation to show the reactants and products.

   | magnesium | + | oxygen | → | magnesium oxide |

[Turn over for Question 2 on *Page twelve*

2. Energy saving light bulbs contain the element mercury which has the atomic number 80.

(a) Circle the correct words to complete the sentence.

Mercury is a {**metal** / non-metal} which is a {gas / **liquid** / solid} at room temperature.   1

(b) The hazard symbol for mercury is:

What does this symbol tell you about mercury?

It is toxic   1

2. **(continued)**

(c) If an energy saving light bulb breaks, mercury vapour escapes into the room. The level of mercury vapour in the room can be calculated using the formula:

$$\text{level of mercury vapour in the room} = \frac{\text{mass of mercury in milligrams}}{\text{volume of room in m}^3}$$

A light bulb containing 4 milligrams of mercury breaks in a room which has a volume of $40\,\text{m}^3$. Calculate the level of mercury vapour in this room.

$4 \div 40 = 0.1$

__0.1__ milligrams per m^3

(3)

[Turn over

3. Many household substances can be classified as acids or alkalis.

   (a) Complete the table to show which of the following substances are acids or alkalis.

   baking soda   lemonade   bleach   vinegar

Acid	Alkali
lemonade	Baking soda
vinegar	bleach

   (b) (i) Diluted hydrochloric acid solution can be neutralised using calcium carbonate.

   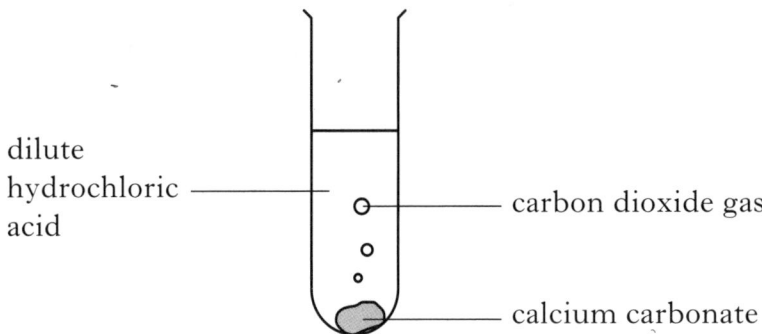

   In this reaction, a calcium salt, water and carbon dioxide gas are formed.

   Name the salt formed in this reaction.

   calcium chloride

   (ii) Indigestion can be caused by too much hydrochloric acid in the stomach. This can be treated using the neutraliser calcium carbonate.

   What would happen to the pH of the acid when calcium carbonate is added?

   it would move closer to 7

4. Tents can be made from a plastic called polyester.

(a) The polyester used is a thermoplastic.

What is meant by a thermoplastic?

Once it has been shaped it cannot be reshaped.

(b) To make the tent waterproof it is coated with a chemical containing silicon.

Write the symbol for silicon.

(You may wish to use page 8 of the data booklet to help you.)

_Si_

(c) Tent poles are often made from aluminium.

What property of aluminium makes it suitable for use as tent poles?

(You may wish to use page 5 of the data booklet to help you.)

low density.

[Turn over

5. Some types of vitamin C tablets fizz when added to water because carbon dioxide gas is produced. A student set up the following experiment to see how long it would take for solution A to turn milky.

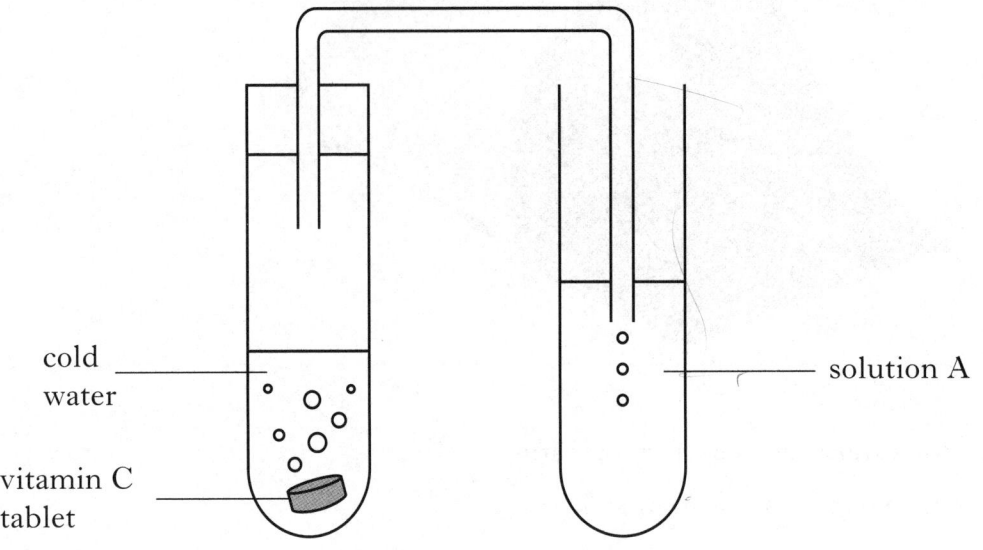

(a) Name solution A.

  Limewater. 1

(b) The experiment was repeated using hot water.

What effect would this have on the time taken for solution A to turn milky?

  It would be faster. 1

(c) Why is it important to have vitamins in our diets?

  to keep us healthy 1

(3)

6. Bridges made from iron need to be protected to stop them from rusting.

(a) What effect would rusting have on the strength of an iron bridge?

It would get weaker

(b) State **one** method that could be used to protect the iron bridge from rusting.

paint

(c) The rate of rusting increases if an iron bridge comes into contact with sea water.

Why does this happen?

Because salt is present. Salt reacts with iron.

(d) An experiment was set up to investigate how iron rusts when it is joined to other metals. Rust indicator turns blue when iron rusts.

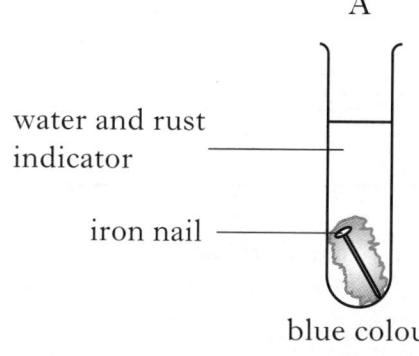
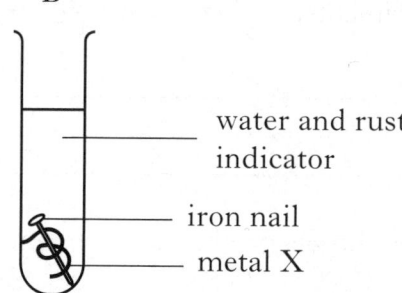

Suggest a name for metal X.

(You may wish to use page 6 of the data booklet to help you.)

zinc

7. The following is taken from the PPA, "Reactions of Metals with Acid".

| Intermediate 1 Chemistry | Reactions of Metals with Acid | Unit 2 PPA 2 |

Procedure (what you do)

1. Add dilute hydrochloric acid to the beaker until it is half full.
2. Put three test tubes in the test tube rack. Pour some of the hydrochloric acid into the first test tube to a depth of about 4 cm. Pour the same volume of acid into the other two test tubes.
3. Add a piece of zinc to the first test tube.
   Add a piece of magnesium to the second test tube.
   Add a piece of copper to the third test tube.

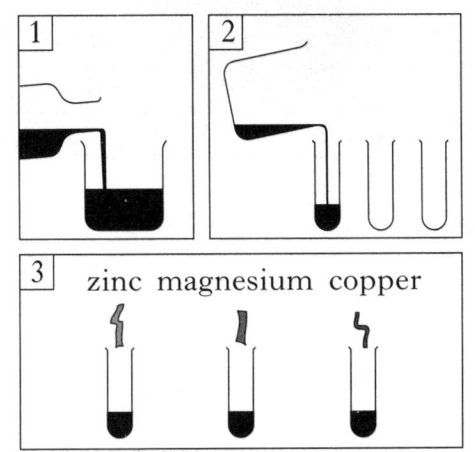

(a) What is the aim of this experiment?

To see which reacts the fastest.

(b) During the experiment the volume of the acid must be kept the same.

State another factor the student must keep the same in each of the three experiments.

The amount of substance added.

(c) Name the gas produced when zinc reacts with hydrochloric acid.

hydrogen

(3)

8. The 2012 Olympic Flame will burn methane, obtained from biogas.

(a) Methane obtained from biogas is a renewable source of energy.

What is meant by a renewable source of energy?

It can be replaced.

(b) Methane is a hydrocarbon.

What is made when a hydrocarbon is burned in a plentiful supply of air?

carbon dioxide and *water*

(c) Biogas is a mixture of gases.

Gases in biogas mixture	Percentage (%)
methane	60
carbon dioxide	25
nitrogen	10
other gases	5

Use the information in the table to label the pie chart.

(An additional pie chart, if required, can be found on *Page twenty-six*).

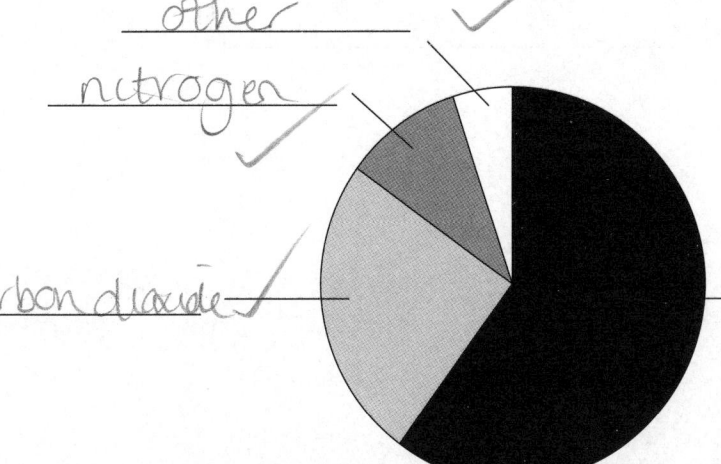

9. During photosynthesis plants take in substances from the environment and, using light energy, make their own food and oxygen.

(a) Name the **two** substances taken in by plants to make their own food.

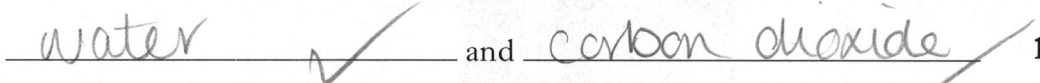

water and carbon dioxide

(b) An experiment was set up. The number of oxygen bubbles produced by a plant in one minute was counted.

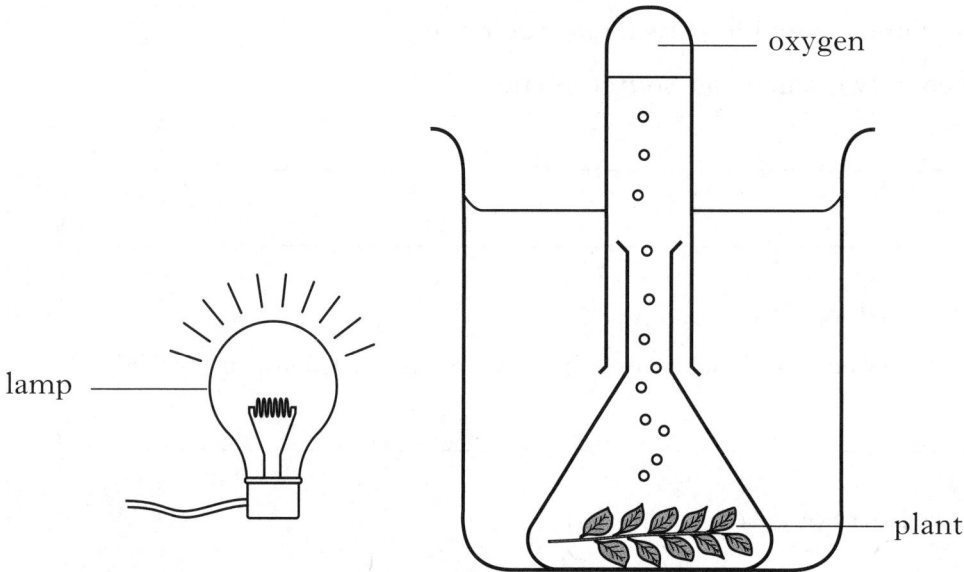

This experiment was repeated with the lamp at different distances from the plant. The results are shown.

Distance of lamp from plant in cm	Number of bubbles of oxygen produced in one minute
30	24
40	19
60	10
100	4

9. (b) (continued)

(i) Circle the correct words to complete the sentence.

As the distance of the lamp from the plant {increases/decreases} the number of bubbles of oxygen gas produced in one minute {increases/decreases}.

decreases is circled in both.

1

(ii) Predict the number of bubbles of oxygen produced if the lamp was 120 cm from the plant.

_____0_____ bubbles

1

(iii) The experiment was repeated to record the volume of oxygen produced.

Name a piece of equipment that could be used to measure the volume of oxygen.

measuring cylinder

1

(c) What is the chemical test for oxygen?

relights a glowing splint

1

(5)

[Turn over

10. Nitrogen is an important element in many fertilisers.

    It is often in the form of nitrate compounds.

    (a) Circle the letter on the diagram to show where the plant takes in nitrate compounds.

    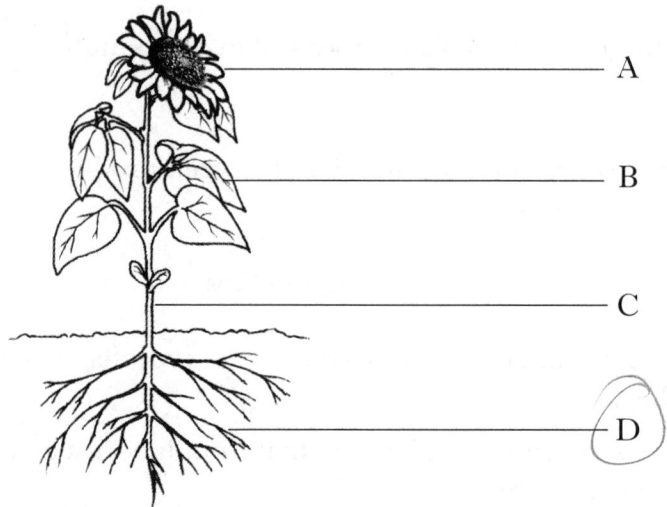

    (b) What effect would harvesting crops have on the levels of nitrogen in the soil?

    Its going to decrease

    (c) A student carried out a PPA to find out which compounds are suitable for use as fertilisers.

    The results are shown.

Name of compound	Suitable for use as fertiliser
ammonium sulphate	yes
ammonium nitrate	yes
calcium phosphate	no
ammonium phosphate	yes

    Why is calcium phosphate **not** suitable for use as a fertiliser?

    because it is insoluble

DO NOT WRITE IN THIS MARGIN

Marks

10. (continued)

(*d*) Overuse of nitrate fertilisers can lead to environmental problems.

Give an example of this.

leaving water lifeless ✓

1

(4)

[Turn over

11. Canoe slalom is an event taking place at this year's Olympics.

(a) As canoe slalom is a power sport, the canoeist needs to ensure he eats enough protein.

What are proteins used for in the body?

growth and repair ✓   1

(b) The protein content of some foods is shown in the table.

Food	Protein per portion in grams
Protein shake	30
Tuna	14
Bagel	9
Milk	9

After a training session the canoeist has a tuna bagel and a glass of milk.

Why is this more beneficial than a protein shake?

As it contains 30g of protien ✓   1

(c) Proteins are formed from amino acids such as glycine, which is shown.

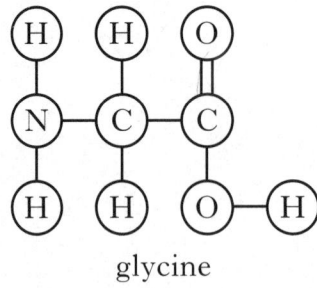

glycine

Complete the formula for this amino acid.

C$_2$H$_5$N$_1$O$_2$ 1

(3)

12. The alcohol, ethanol, is added to some mouthwashes to kill bacteria in the mouth.

(a) The table shows the ethanol content of different mouthwashes.

Mouthwash	Ethanol content (%)
Ice	7
Zing	14
Gleam	19
Sparkle	27

Use the information in the table to draw a bar graph.

(Additional graph paper, if required, can be found on *Page twenty-six*.)

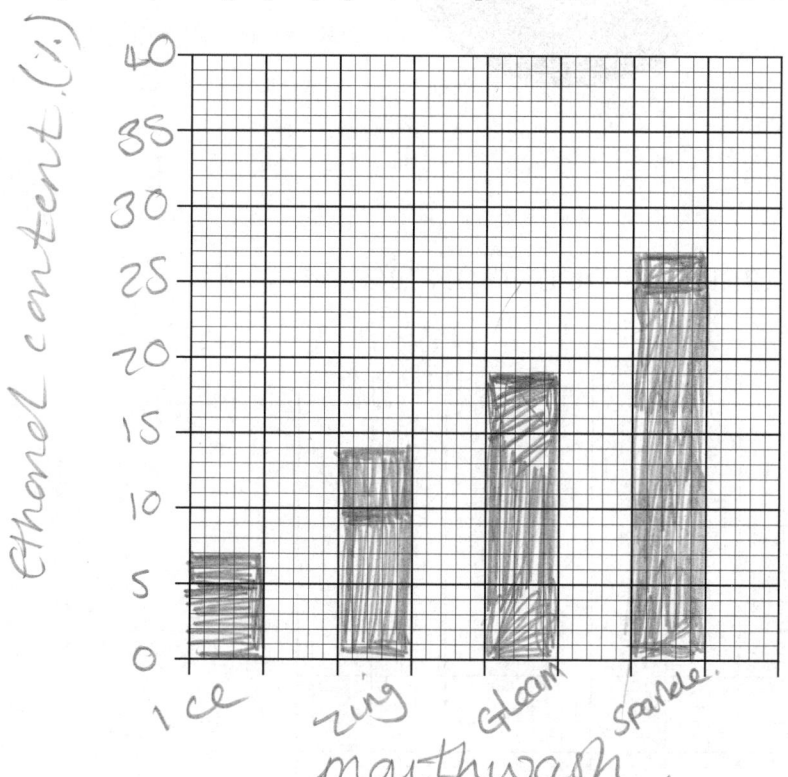

(b) All alcohols kill bacteria.

Why must the alcohol, methanol, **not** be used in mouthwash?

It is toxic

(c) Some mouthwashes also contain sodium fluoride.

Suggest a reason for this.

protects teeth

[END OF QUESTION PAPER]

ADDITIONAL SPACE FOR ANSWERS

ADDITIONAL PIE CHART FOR QUESTION 8(c).

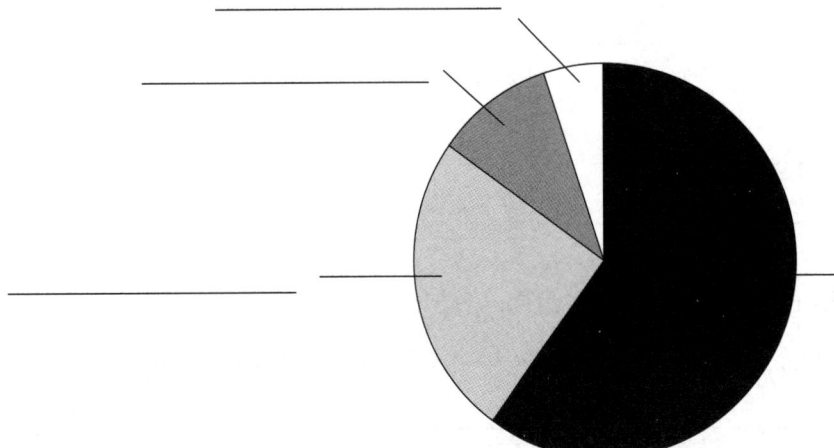

ADDITIONAL GRAPH PAPER FOR QUESTION 12(a).

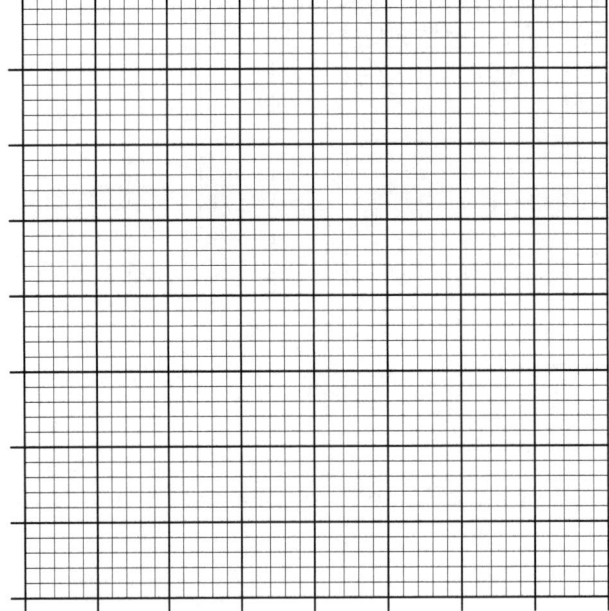

ADDITIONAL SPACE FOR ANSWERS

ADDITIONAL SPACE FOR ANSWERS

Acknowledgements

Permission has been sought from all relevant copyright holders and Bright Red Publishing is grateful for the use of the following:

A photograph of European Airbus A300–600 © Airbus SAS/Airbus UK (2008 page 14);

An extract adapted from the article 'In the Mix' © FAIA (2008 page 22);

A photograph of Rolawn GroRight fertiliser reproduced with permission of Rolawn Limited (2010 page 20);

A photograph of a BMW Clean Energy car © BMW (2011 page 13);

An extract from the poem 'When the world was sad' by Rachel Farnsworth, winner of the Royal Society of Chemistry Bill Bryson prize © Rachel Farnsworth (2011 page 16);

The 2012 Olympic logo © LOCOG (2012 page 19).

INTERMEDIATE 1 | ANSWER SECTION

CHEMISTRY INTERMEDIATE 1
2008

SECTION A

1. C	11. A
2. A	12. C
3. D	13. A
4. B	14. C
5. C	15. B
6. A	16. D
7. A	17. B
8. D	18. D
9. B	19. C
10. D	20. A

SECTION B

1. (a) Mg

   (b) Carbon; C

   (c) Number of protons: 11

   Mass number: 23

2. (a) Sodium (Na)/Oxygen (O)

   (b) Propene (propylene)

   (c) Chlorine; Cl

3. (a) B D A C

   (b) (i) Place (the test-tube) in a beaker of hot water/Place in water bath

   (ii) Any one from:
   - orange/red
   - brown/orange
   - yellow/orange
   - green/orange
   - brick orange

4. (a) Silicon/Si

   (b) Low density/light/lightweight

   (c) (i) The bulb would light/switch on/turn on/light/glow

   (ii) sulphur: Non-conductor

   tin: Conductor

5. (a) hydrocarbon

   (b) (i) C_8H_8

   (ii) Has a much higher melting point

6. (a) They dissolve grease/forms a lather/separates grease

   Using laureth sulphates

   (b) pH 1–6/pH < 7

   (c) Any one from:
   - Sodium laureth sulphate
   - Magnesium laureth sulphate
   - Aqua laureth sulphate
   - laureth sulphate

7. (a) Oxygen/O/O_2

   (b) (i) It has the highest %age of carbon.

   (ii) $\frac{90}{100} \times 200 = 180$ kg

   (c) They cannot be replaced/cannot be remade/run out/won't last forever.

8. (a) 10

   (b) (i) B

   (ii) Waste plant material

   (c) (i) Any one from:
   - plastic
   - glass
   - paper
   - metal tins
   - plant material (compost)
   - clothes
   - ink catridges

   (or other reasonable answer)

   (ii) methane/biogas/natural gas

9. (a) Any one from:
   - prolong shelf-life
   - makes food last longer
   - not spoil (go bad) as quickly
   - prevents bugs/micro-organisms from growing

   (b) Sorbic acid

   (c) hydrocarbons

   (d) $SO_2/S_1O_2/O_2S$

10. (a) (i) Provide energy/respiration can take place

    (ii) Any one from:
    - to reduce the chance of heart disease
    - reduce obesity
    - prevent clogged arteries
    - stop you getting fat
    - strokes
    - high blood pressure

    (b) (i) Any one from:
    - to keep the gut working well
    - helps pass food through gut
    - make you go to the toilet

    (ii) 3·6g

11. (a) Light energy (sunlight)/sun/solar

    (b) Carbon dioxide/CO_2

    (c) Decreases/gets smaller/goes down/falls

CHEMISTRY INTERMEDIATE 1
2009

SECTION A

1.	D	11.	A
2.	A	12.	D
3.	C	13.	B
4.	B	14.	D
5.	A	15.	A
6.	C	16.	C
7.	A	17.	B
8.	C	18.	C
9.	B	19.	A
10.	D	20.	D

SECTION B

1. (a) O_3

    (b) Toxic/Poisonous
    Harmful/irritant

    (c) (Sunscreen) 3

2. (a) Mass/weight of salt in grams

    (b) $(101 - 100) = 1°C$

    (c) Saturated

3. (a) Wine and lemonade

    (b) (Black) coffee

    (c) (i) A solid/powder (at the bottom of the test-tube)/Saw a precipitate/crystals

    (ii) Nitric (acid)

4. (a) Sodium carbonate

    Hydrochloric acid

    Carbon dioxide

    (b) (i) Oxygen

    (ii) Combustion

5. (a) (Fractional) distillation

    (b) carbon and hydrogen

    (c) lower
    smaller

    (d) $(100 - 65) = 35\%$

6. (a) alloys

    (b) (i) It decreases

    (ii) 191-226 inclusive

    (c) Lead is toxic/poisonous/harmful

7. (a) (Oxygen) will relight a glowing splint

    (b) (i) Very bright glow

    (ii) *Any one of:*
    Mercury/gold/silver/platinum

8. (a) By changing the number of drops of detergent added

    (b) To obtain accurate/reliable results

    (c) Scum

9. (a) Calcium

    (b) (i) (Vitamin) C (Vitamin) A (Vitamin) B2/(Vitamin) D
    (Vitamin) B

    (ii) (Vitamin) D (Vitamin) A

10. (a) (The effect of) temperature/heat

    (b) Enzyme/yeast does not work (at 60°C)

11. (a) Thermometer

    (b) The test-tubes/spoons (or burning carbohydrates) are at different heights

12. (a) (i) Phosphorous or P

    (ii) Label on y-axis percentage or %
    Bars correctly identified with symbols or abbreviations
    Scale on y-axis

    (b) Blue
    Purple

    (c) Rub onto (filter) paper – leaves a greasy/transparent/translucent mark

CHEMISTRY INTERMEDIATE 1
2010

SECTION A

1.	B	11.	B
2.	D	12.	A
3.	C	13.	C
4.	A	14.	B
5.	D	15.	B
6.	A	16.	C
7.	D	17.	C
8.	A	18.	A
9.	D	19.	C
10.	B	20.	B

SECTION B

1. (a) Hg

    (b) Metal

    (c) thermometer/dental amalgam/barometer

2. (a) Circle corrosive symbol

    (b) (i) 5

      (ii) LHS = paints or 20%
      Top RHS = fertilisers or 35%
      Bottom RHS = fibres or 10%

3. (a) Bubbles of gas/
    Fizzing/
    Effervescence/
    Colour change/
    Change in appearance/
    Energy change/gets hot/flame produced
    Gas given off
    Gas produced is flammable
    New substance/ product/ chemical made
    Reactants used up

    (b) *All three required*:
    Calcium carbide + water → acetylene

    (c) Quicker/faster/speeds up/increases

4. (a) (body) growth and repair
    Repair/building muscle (and tissues)
    Build up muscles (and bones/ heart/cells)

    (b) (i) C_3 H_9 N_1
      (ii) Molecule

5. (a) Lead and bromine/
    Pb and Br

    (b) High and strong

    (c) A

6. (a) (Zinc) <u>chloride</u>

    (b) Burns with a (squeaky)pop/
    Lighted splint pops

    (c) Less bubbles/
    Less gas
    Less hydrogen made

7. (a) Alloy

    (b)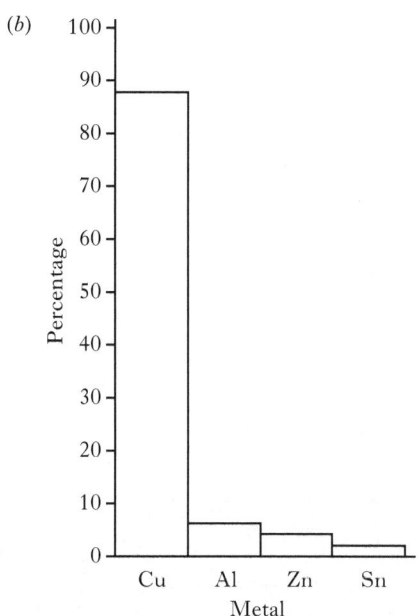

8. (a) Oxygen

    (b) (i) Blue
      (ii) C

9. (a) Oil/Gas/Peat

    (b) Plant remains

    (c) Turns milky/
      chalky/
      cloudy/

10. (a) Cracking

    (b) Polyethene/
    Poly(ethene)

    (c) Can be reshaped on heating/shaped on heating
    Melted and reshaped

11. (a) Phosphorous/P

    (b) (Very) soluble

    (c) Beans/clover

12. (a) B → D → E → A → C

    (b) Mass of carbohydrate/ flour/ icing sugar
    Distance burning spoon from test-tube/
    Same (size of) test tube
    Same (size of) burning spoon
    Weight of carbohydrate/icing sugar/flour

13. (a) 26

    (b) Sucrose/glucose/fructose/maltose

    (c) Heart disease
    Heart attacks
    Heart problems
    Angina
    Get fat/obese
    Strokes
    Clogs/blocks arteries
    High blood pressure
    Cardiovascular problems
    Overweight

14. (a) (i) Alter the flavour/
    Tastes better/worse
    Improve the keeping qualities/
    Lasts longer/
    Supply nutrition/
    Enhance nutrition/
    Change colour/appearance
    (ii) 1/10 × 100
    = 10%

    (b) Antibiotic

CHEMISTRY INTERMEDIATE 1
2011

SECTION A

1.	D	11.	C
2.	B	12.	A
3.	D	13.	C
4.	C	14.	B
5.	C	15.	B
6.	A	16.	D
7.	C	17.	A
8.	A	18.	D
9.	D	19.	C
10.	B	20.	A

SECTION B

1. (a) non-metals

   (b) helium/He
   neon/Ne
   xenon/Xe
   radon/Rn
   kryptn/Kr

   (c) To prevent tooth decay/
   strengthen teeth/
   keep teeth healthy/
   provides toothcare/
   helps teeth/
   any suggestion of protecting teeth

2. (a) To speed up a reaction

   (b) (i) Manganese dioxide/manganese oxide

   (ii) *Any two from:*
   (same) mass of catalyst
   (same) volume of hydrogen peroxide (+detergent)
   (same) concentration of hydrogen peroxide
   (same) temperature of hydrogen peroxide
   (same) time for lather to form/rise up measuring cylinder
   (same) volume of detergent
   (same) size particles
   catalyst used same size
   same amount of chemicals/solution
   2g catalyst used
   20cm^3 of hydrogen peroxide + detergent
   30secs each time
   time
   (same) type of detergent

   (iii) Relights a glowing splint

3. (a) Change of colour/
   New substance forms
   new product formed/change of appearance
   copper turned green/cannot see any copper
   copper disappears
   (green) copper ethanoate forms/is made

   (b) Oxygen/
   O/
   O$_2$

   (c) Prevents disease/bacteria/fungi/infections/mould
   Stops disease
   Kills/removes disease

OFFICIAL SQA ANSWERS TO INTERMEDIATE 1 CHEMISTRY

4. (a) Dip pH paper in solution
   and
   Compare (colour) to chart

   (b) (i) E

   (ii) Alkali

5. (a) To complete the circuit

   (b) increase/
   rise/
   get higher

   (c) chemicals get used (up)/
   zinc/copper/silver oxide/magnesium gets used (up)
   solution/ions get used up/run out
   acid runs out
   chemicals/substances used up/run out
   all chemical reactions have taken place/finished

6. (a) hydrogen + oxygen ⟶ water (hydrogen oxide)
   or
   oxygen + hydrogen ⟶ water
   or
   $H_2 + O_2 \longrightarrow H_2O$

   (b) It is (very) flammable/
   It can explode/
   It can burst into flames

   (c) 2.5×50
   $= 125$

7. (a) (i) Alloy

   (ii) LHS = copper/Cu/60
   Top RHS = zinc/Zn/25
   Bottom RHS = nickel/Ni/15

   (b) Thermoplastic

8. (a) (i) Plant (remains)/trees/vegetation/wood

   (ii) Limited supply/runs out/is running out/cannot be replaced/not renewable/won't last forever/once used up there is no more

   (b) (i) increases/goes up/rises/gets higher/greater/more kj

   (ii) Ethane/
   C_2H_6

9. (a) Greenhouse effect/greenhouse process/greenhouse (gas)
   Global warming

   (b) (Increased) burning of fuels/fossil fuels
   Cutting down of forests/deforestation
   too much fuel burnt
   (more) cars/more people driving/vehicles

   (c) Glucose (made)
   Oxygen (made)

10. (a) (i) Energy

    (ii) increases/rises up/goes up/gets higher

    (b) Iodine/I/I_2

    (c) (i) Speed increases/
    Gets faster/
    Gets quicker

    (ii) Any value above 37 but lower than 64

    (iii) Blue to red/orange/brown/yellow/green

11. (a) $175 \times 12/1000$
    $= 2.1$ units

    (b) 3 hours

(c)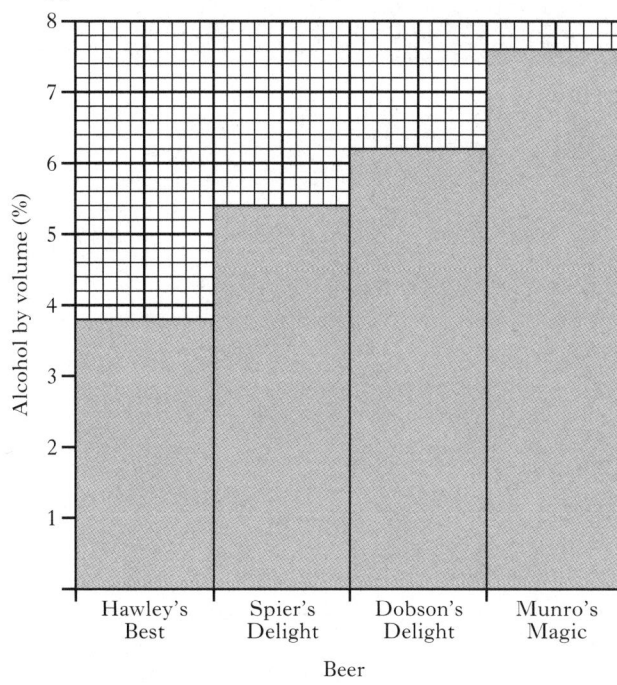

(d) *Any one from:*
Supply/enhance nutritional value of food, enhance vitamin content
Suggestion of changing the appearance of food eg colour
Suggestion of changing the flavour of food

CHEMISTRY INTERMEDIATE 1 2012

SECTION A

1.	D	11.	A
2.	A	12.	D
3.	B	13.	A
4.	C	14.	C
5.	D	15.	B
6.	B	16.	B
7.	C	17.	D
8.	D	18.	C
9.	A	19.	C
10.	B	20.	A

SECTION B

1. (a) Lithium, carbon and oxygen
    or
    Li, C or O/O_2

   (b) magnesium + oxygen ⟶ magnesium oxide
    or
    oxygen + magnesium ⟶ magnesium oxide

2. (a) ½ mark for Metal
    ½ mark for Liquid

   (b) Toxic/poisonous

   (c) 0.1

3. (a)

Acid	Alkali
vinegar	bleach
lemonade	baking soda

   (b) (i) Chloride

    (ii) increases/
    moves towards 7/
    becomes neutral/
    acidity decreases/
    will neutralise (the acid)

4. (a) Reshaped on heating/
    Melts and can be reshaped/
    Can be heated and shaped and when reheated returns to original shape/

   (b) Si

   (c) Low density/
    Lightweight
    Strong/

5. (a) Lime water

   (b) Less (time)
    Faster/quicker <u>time</u>

   (c) Keeps the body healthy/
    Keep body working properly/
    Body functions better/properly/
    Prevents diseases/
    Healthy body growth/
    Helps immune system

6. (a) Decreases/
    Weakens/
    Less strong

   (b) Painting/
    Greasing/
    Electroplating/
    Galvanising/zinc coating
    Tin-plating/
    Sacrificial protection/
    Attach to a more reactive metal/
    Attach magnesium/
    Plastic-coating/
    Varnish/
    Coat it with a substance that is waterproof/ or implication that it is waterproof
    Dip coating/
    Oiling/
    Any metal coating (not Hg/K/Li/Na/Ca)

   (c) Salt (is present)/
    Ions (are present)
    or
    Salt reacts with iron to make it rust/
    Salt reacts with metal

   (d) Zinc/
    Aluminium/
    Magnesium

7. (a) To place the metals in order of reactivity/corrosion/
    To find out the reactivity of zinc, magnesium and copper/
    To find out how reactive the metals are/
    To see which metals react with acid and which don't/
    To see which metals corrode fastest/
    To see what/how metals react with acid

   (b) Concentration (of acid)/
    Temperature (of acid)/
    Size/length of metal/
    Mass/weight (of metal)/
    Type of acid/
    Amount of time (in acid)/
    Specified temperature

   (c) Hydrogen/
    H/
    H_2

8. (a) They can be replaced/re-made/re-creacted/more can be made quickly/reproduced

   (b) ½ mark for carbon dioxide
    ½ mark for water

   (c)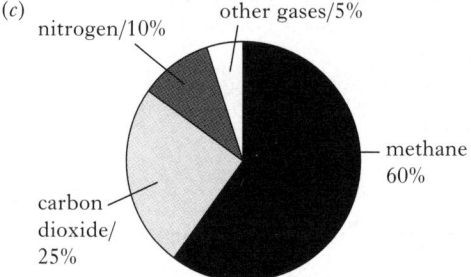

9. (a) ½ mark for carbon dioxide
    ½ mark for water

OFFICIAL SQA ANSWERS TO INTERMEDIATE 1 CHEMISTRY

(b) (i) Increases and decreases
  or
  Decreases and increases

  (ii) Less than 4
  0 included

  (iii) Syringe/
  Measuring cylinder/tube/beaker
  Ruler (and test-tube)
  burette

(c) Relights a glowing splint

10. (a) D

(b) Reduces/
Lowers/
Gets less/
Decreases/
Not be enough left

(c) Insoluble/
Not soluble
or
Doesn't dissolve in water

(d) Leave water lifeless/
Kills/harms fish/animals
or
Algae bloom/
Poisons water/lakes
or
Reduces oxygen levels in water
or
Contaminates wildlife

11. (a) For growth and repair/
For growth/
For repair/heal
Repair damaged tissues/muscles
Mending tissues/heal wounds
Muscles
tissue

(b) More protein/
Has 32 grams of protein/
Will have 2 grams more of protein/
Has more grams of protein

(c) $C_2H_5N_1O_2$/
$C_2H_5NO_2$

12. (a)
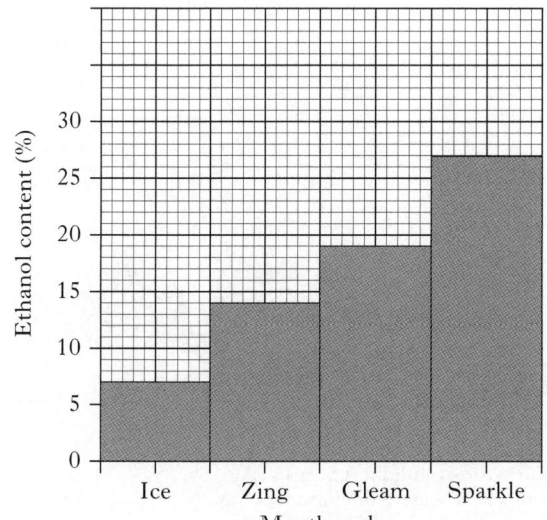

½ mark for ethanol content **and** (%) label
½ mark for scale on ethanol content axis
½ mark for bars labelled (x-axis label not required)
½ mark for correct height of bars

(b) Poisonous/
Toxic/
Causes blindness/
Can kill/
Causes death

(c) Prevents tooth decay/
Protects teeth/
Keeps teeth strong

Hey! I've done it

© 2012 SQA/Bright Red Publishing Ltd, All Rights Reserved
Published by Bright Red Publishing Ltd, 6 Stafford Street, Edinburgh, EH3 7AU
Tel: 0131 220 5804, Fax: 0131 220 6710, enquiries: sales@brightredpublishing.co.uk,
www.brightredpublishing.co.uk

Official SQA answers to 978-1-84948-261-5
2008-2012